WESTCHESTER BURNING

WESTCHESTER BURNING

Portrait of a Marriage

Amine Wefali

The Dial Press

Published by
THE DIAL PRESS
Random House, Inc.
1540 Broadway
New York, New York 10036

LIBRARY OF CONGRESS CATALOGING IN PUBLICATION DATA
Wefali, Amine.
   Westchester burning / Amine Wefali.
     p. cm.
   ISBN 0-385-33511-3
   1. Wefali, Amine. 2. Wives—Biography.
3. Divorced women—Biography. I. Title.
HQ734.W4355 2002
306.872'092—dc21
[B]   2001059868

Book design by Sabrina Bowers

Manufactured in the United States of America
Published simultaneously in Canada

July 2002

10   9   8   7   6   5   4   3   2   1
BVG

Author's Note

Certain characters, places, and events in this book are composite sketches of people I know, places I've been, and events in my life. I have changed everyone's name except my own, and in some cases, I have changed certain identifying characteristics of individuals to protect their privacy.

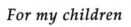

For my children

WESTCHESTER BURNING

Smile

Madison Avenue was wet and cold. The first snow of the winter disappeared as it hit the pavement. It wasn't a retrospective, Susan said, just some photographs her husband put together, representing his work through four decades.

As I walked in, I saw Dooley. He and Leslie lived in the town we left. Dooley told me it was always so wonderful to see me, that Martin and he went to Yale, that they and their wives try to get together at least twice a year, that it's always so much fun. I smiled and said that's wonderful.

"I hear you and Phillip are moving back to Westchester."

I smiled. If he knew that, he probably knew the rest. Leslie came over, said hello, and told her husband she wanted him to see something.

I stood before a large black and white photograph. A dark-haired girl sitting, holding on to her cigarette. A boy, his head raised, lies beside her. The Coney Island boardwalk stretches out behind them into a summer haze.

"Isn't it amazing how close they let him come in?" a stranger beside me said.

"He was probably their age when he took it," I replied.

"Of course," and the stranger laughed. "May I ask where you were then?"

"I was riding my bicycle to the Nyack library to sneak in to read Nancy Drew and *The Secret of the Girl Who Couldn't Remember*. And you?"

"Stationed in Germany with Elvis."

It was then I saw him.

He walked by, his hand holding hers, guiding their way through the crowd. She was young and thin. Her thick, curly dark hair was held together by pins.

Had he cleared up her face the same way he cleared up my weight? Was he in awe of her? Did he serve her tea sweetened with rose-petal jam in his darkened office? And did he tell her, softly, to bend lower as he entered her from behind?

I moved to the bar, and a young man gave me my vodka with no ice in a wineglass, and I made my way to where they stood.

My hand reached out and touched the back of his jacket.

He turned and looked at me with no surprise.

"Hello. Martin lives in our building."

"Who's Martin?"

"He's the photographer. We're at his show."

"You're still in the city?"

I turned away.

On my way out I passed the stranger leaning against a pillar. And we smiled.

Dress Rehearsal

We moved to New York in the late spring of 1969. Our first apartment was in Brooklyn Heights on the ground floor of a brownstone. The kitchen, bathroom were windowless, the living room, bedroom faced a large sunlit garden. Phillip had been offered a position with a Wall Street firm before graduating from Stanford, and I found a job as a receptionist for three radiologists half a block from the Metropolitan Museum of Art. One night on the way home I saw a hundred leather-bound volumes neatly stacked at the curb of the limestone townhouse near where I worked. I couldn't get in touch with Phillip and took the books before someone else did. The cabdriver helped me put them in the taxi and helped me unload them in front of our curb. Phillip said they were worthless and I stacked them neatly by the wall next to the fireplace, where they stayed for a few years, until they were finally thrown out.

I took a bookkeeping course and worked for a sportswear manufacturer on West Thirty-Eighth Street. If I took my lunch hour, I spent it on the main floor of Lord & Taylor. The salesladies at the cosmetics counters and I talked about creams, perfumes, and President Nixon. They gave me samples and tried to talk me into free makeup sessions. My mother told me never to wear makeup, it aged the skin; all you needed was a good moisturizer and a rich night cream. Once I bought a pair of brown leather gloves I couldn't afford. At my desk, when I took them out of the tissue paper, I saw they were spotted. The saleslady refused to take them back. She said there was nothing wrong with them. I again told her they had spots. She said they didn't and called over her supervisor, and when he didn't see the spots, I started to cry. On the subway ride to Brooklyn, I thought the reason why I saw the spots and they didn't was because the office I sat in was lit with fluorescent bulbs, and Lord & Taylor had lamps on their counters. When Phillip came in, I told him what had happened and again I started to cry. He didn't say anything.

A week later, at work, I got a phone call from the secretary to the president of Lord & Taylor. She said my husband had called, and they would of course take the gloves back.

Phillip and I were married a year later at the municipal building. My mother told Phillip he should volunteer to be the witness for the couple ahead of us. The woman wore a sable coat, and the man was asked to prove his age. A sign posted by the staircase said it was dangerous to throw rice. My mother gave me a strand of pearls she said was for my twenty-third birthday in May. I was to always wear them against my skin. The oil from my skin would give the pearls their luster and she and my sister Natalie flew back to California.

Phillip usually worked late, and I started working late. We tried having dinner together. We'd have a couple of nightcaps, be in bed by two, and be up at seven to go to work. When we had parties, they'd start Friday night, and it wouldn't be unusual for a few of our friends to sleep on the couch or on the floor and have Bloody Marys with us in the morning.

We planned a trip to Europe to buy a motorcycle, and to save money we'd stay in campgrounds. We bought a sleeping bag, a one-man tent, and a parachute to keep our clothes in from an army-navy store on Canal Street. My father told us Germany could be wet and cold in the summer. We didn't listen.

We'd never been on a motorcycle, and I watched Phillip drive around the lot of the BMW factory a few times before getting on with our things. The motorcyclists who passed us, as we drove on the shoulder of the roads, were outfitted in black leather. I folded our towel and put it under Phillip's sweater against his chest and kept my face hidden against his back as we rode. There's a photograph I took of Phillip by Starnberger See. I told him he looked like Omar Sharif in *Dr. Zhivago*.

We paid extra to have the motorcycle brought by plane so we wouldn't miss the New England fall, and we picked it up from JFK, at night, a few weeks after we flew back from Amsterdam. On the Grand Central Parkway, a man in the backseat of a limo opened his window and reached out and touched me. Phillip swerved into the next lane, and a truck almost hit us. We left the motorcycle in the garage across the street, where it stayed until a first-year associate from Phillip's firm bought it.

Two years later we bought a midnight blue 911T Porsche, using the thousand dollars we were saving for an apartment as a down payment for the car. We kept it in my father's garage, and we took the bus to Nyack to drive it around. My mother called to say, who did I think I was garaging a car in that bastard's garage? If I couldn't afford to garage a car, I had no business owning one.

I got pregnant on our fifth wedding anniversary and miscarried three months later. It was the only time I saw Phillip cry. He took me to Bermuda, and I got pregnant with Michael. I couldn't stand the smell of alcohol, and Phillip started drinking alone.

We bought a co-op on West Ninety-Third Street. Phillip painted the apartment and sanded the floors during his vacation while Michael and I stayed in Nyack for the month. My father and Rosa were in Istanbul visiting her family. Natalie flew in from Los Angeles to help me with Michael; I was fourteen when she was born and now she was fourteen.

Phillip bought the crib we had picked out on a Sunday walk down Third Avenue and placed it near our bed, and he painted the wicker rocking chair Rosa gave us, and he picked up the cushions for it from the seamstress who had her shop above the butcher's on Montague Street.

I never allowed Michael to be alone. When I went to the bathroom or took a shower, I told Natalie to sit on the bed next to his bassinet and not to take her eyes off him. In September when Natalie had to go back to Los Angeles, I couldn't go into the room where she had slept, I'd start to cry. She forgot a pair of shoes, and I wore them instead of sending them to her.

In the late afternoon, if it was raining or snowing, Michael and I would go to the basement playroom. He would build cities with large red and white paper blocks, and I talked to whoever was down there. I was elected chairman of our block's sanitation committee, and every Saturday morning a group of us would meet and sweep both sides of the block from Broadway to West End Avenue. The super of our building used a wrench to open the fire hydrant, and by noon our street was clean. Diana and her husband David were one of the few couples who were there every Saturday, and we became friends.

Michael and I were in the elevator one morning on our way to the park, he wanted to ride the plastic motorcycle Phillip had bought him for his second birthday, when Diana walked in. I asked her how David and the girls were, and she told me David wanted to leave. He said he had to have quiet to write his dissertation and she started to cry. We went back up to our apartment. I let Michael play with a bowl of eggs, and I made a pot of strong black tea with milk and honey for Diana and myself. I told her we were going to start going to the movies, and afterward we'd go somewhere for dessert, and we'd go to a different place every time. "You can bring your girls over. This way we'll only need one sitter." Diana and I were in a baby-sitting club, there were about fifty of us. During the daytime the child came to you, and if it was at night, you would go to the child's apartment. You were paid with a hollow coin, each one worth an hour. At the Christmas Hanukkah party in the lobby, Diana and I asked Mr. Seville, whose wife had left him, if he would like to join us? He told us he didn't like going to the movies, but he would like to take us out to dinner. And he did, every Wednesday. He was the first cellist of the Metropolitan Opera, and he gave Diana and me tickets to the dress rehearsals.

Phillip worked eighty-hour weeks on a three-hundred-million-dollar utility restructuring. The closing went well, and a vice president involved in the deal was promoted. When she left the bank to go to an investment firm, she told her boss they had to use Phillip. Phillip started bringing in a lot of money for the firm, and he was made partner. Coming home from a function held in his honor, Phillip said all he did was make money for people who already had it.

We had our apartment painted, the kitchen updated, and the windows measured for shutters. The car was now garaged a street away, and we bought an antique French country table and six chairs for the yellow dining room.

Rolls of Pennies

Michael was three and ready for nursery school. Diana's girls were in the first grade at Nightingale-Bamford. She told me we should try getting Michael into Horace Mann or Trinity. I wanted a less pressured environment for him and convinced Phillip to have Michael go to Walden.

I was pregnant with Katherine, and Michael and I were walking up Broadway. He was holding my hand when I was knocked to the ground by a heavily medicated young man living in a single-room-occupancy building next door to us.

Phillip thought it was time we left the city. We looked at a house on a quiet street in a town in Westchester. Phillip thought the house was too small. He said he didn't want to be sitting on something the minute he walked in. I convinced him to buy the house. It was small, but it was lovely, and nothing had to be done to it.

We sold our co-op. Diana organized a good-bye party, and I

gave her all the baby-sitting coins I had accumulated. Mr. Seville sent me two dozen long-stem yellow roses.

We bought a golden retriever puppy for Michael in New Jersey. While driving back across the George Washington Bridge, I asked Michael what name he would give her. He said, "Bridge," and I added an "s."

Phillip agreed Michael should continue at Walden until after the New Year. In the mornings, Phillip, Michael, and I drove to the city in the car. I stopped taking walks through Central Park or quickly catching a photography exhibit. Instead, I told Diana I was too tired, and I waited for Michael in the car in front of Walden, eating a loaf of sliced black bread.

One morning the windshield of the car shattered as we were driving in on the Henry Hudson Parkway. Philip thought someone had thrown a rock at us, and I thought we must have run over something that bounced up onto our windshield. Phillip told me to go to the police, after I dropped Michael off, to fill out a report for the insurance company.

When I picked Michael up at twelve, it was raining. I didn't put the windshield wipers on, I was afraid the movement of the blades would cause the shattered glass to come apart and fall inside the car. Keeping my head out the window, it took me three hours to drive from the city to the house. I left the car by the garage with its door open and Michael sleeping in the back. The baby had dropped and was pressing against my bladder. All three doors were locked, and I had left the keys inside. I squatted in front of the house, under the larger holly tree.

With one of the fire logs stacked at the side of the house, I broke a window and wiped the blood from my hand against the wet fur of the beaver coat Phillip's mother had left me in her will. I carried Michael in and laid him on the living-room couch. I let Bridges out, cleaned up after her, and made Michael something to eat, and as he watched *Sesame Street*, I went out to put the car in the garage and backed it into the drainage ditch that ran alongside the driveway. The back tires just dug in deeper. I called for a tow truck, asking them to please come before my husband got home. At eight the man got the car out and asked for twenty-five dollars. I told him I didn't have any money and apologized when I gave him sixty rolls of pennies Michael and I had spent a few afternoons making. The man said it was OK. One lady, once, gave him a jar of coins; mine were at least wrapped. He asked if my husband was interested in selling his Porsche.

"What's wrong with you?" Phillip said when he came into the kitchen, snow lightly sprinkled on the brim of his brown felt hat and on the shoulders of his dark blue cashmere coat.

"I want to move back to New York."

"Are you kidding?"

I pointed to his dinner on the stove and climbed the stairs to bed.

Widows

"I'm not sending out invitations. Just put away October twenty-first, at night. I figure if I made it the twenty-first at the '21' Club, everyone will remember. If you wear black, I'm throwing you out. I'll probably be spending the next one in the nursing home, so I want this one to be really good."

I wore a V-neck black silk crepe dress that went to midcalf and blue suede shoes with a two-inch heel. I decided not to wear stockings.

A group of us sat at the banquette near the bar. We were offered a glass of champagne and spiced beef on a stick. I asked for hot water with lemon and thought of the time I worked a party for the Westchester Arts Council. About eight hundred people showed up, and I stood among them under the vaulted ceiling of the converted bank holding a thick ceramic plate of crabmeat, eel, and tuna sushi. Some people asked what was in the sushi and whether they should have it, others took a piece without saying anything, and some ignored me. I'd walk behind a black curtain to a makeshift kitchen to replenish the plate, and on the way out I'd pass an artist whose installation of a toilet seat entitled "Don't Look at What's Inside" kept falling off the wall.

The birthday girl finally arrived in yellow strapless satin, a white fox boa, and a tiara. The slit of her dress went to the top of her thigh, shimmering gold stockings, gold high heel sandals. Her cheeks were flushed, and she had a big smile. We applauded. She did a short mock striptease, and everyone laughed.

"I will have my champagne at the table. Girls, follow me."

In a line we followed her to the back of a dining room, through the kitchen, down a flight of steep steps, through a small office, over a high step into a long, narrow, dimly lit room.

Originally the "21" Club was in one townhouse. During Prohibition the liquor was kept in the basement of the townhouse next door. We were dining in that basement. The walls were lined in racks of wine. In the middle of a long table, the number 21 and two jockeys on either side were inlaid, the 21 in black and the jockeys in colors. A white linen placemat with napkin, five crystal glasses of various sizes, a Limoges plate, and silver service for a seven-course meal were placed in front of each of the twenty upholstered chairs. Seven waiters stood at attention. There was a collective intake of breath. The Pointer Sisters were singing on a CD one of the women brought.

Carole kissed me and handed me a box with a pink silk ribbon: a paisley woven cashmere shawl in pale pastels. "Just shut up and put it on. I knew you'd wear fucking black."

We joined hands and sang "God Bless America." Carole said Giuliani told everyone to start spending money, and "boy am I doing it. I'm not leaving anything behind except for the corpse and I guess my new teeth, which, by the way, cost more than this table. I told Eloise to bury me naked."

I sat on her right, and her new friend from Nantucket sat on her left. She kept referring to herself and to her friend as "the widows." Finally I asked what was with this widows thing.

She leaned over, "Men marry widows. They never marry divorcées."

In the Middle of an Apple Orchard

In the mornings I walked on the main road to town to buy food for dinner. I'd push Katherine in her carriage, and Michael tried to keep up, Bridges alongside of him, making sure he stayed to the side of the road. I never met anyone. Diana would call, I'd tell her I had to go, that I'd call her back, and didn't.

In the afternoons, I'd bundle Michael up and tell him to go play outside. I could watch him through the windows.

Charlotte was born when Katherine was sixteen months. I had three children under the age of five, and I rarely got out of my bathrobe. I was thirty-three years old.

We chose our town for its school system, but when Michael came home from kindergarten one afternoon crying, telling me he was stupid, I looked at a Montessori school in Greenwich, thirteen miles from our house. Phillip liked the school, and when Katherine turned three, she went there too.

When Charlotte was ready for nursery school, I told Phillip I really wanted to move back to the city. He told me the city was not for kids. I told him we had to make the house bigger. He told me to go ahead. I told him we should look for a bigger house. He told me to go look.

"Mrs. Calt, I have the perfect house for you. You're going to love it. It's the big Victorian on Sheppard Road, and Whispering Pines is the elementary." Our town had three elementary schools, and Whispering Pines was the most desired.

"Mrs. Lester, I've seen it."

It was one of the first houses I was shown when I started looking. The wall and floors were painted black. A billiard table took up the dining room. Empty bottles of Dom Perignon stood on the narrow edge of wainscoting running throughout the downstairs rooms. Tall pines surrounded it.

"Mrs. Calt. It's been completely redone by the new owners. They've only been in it for a couple of months. They're moving back to Chicago. He's taking over the family business. Your husband is going to love it."

Mrs. Lester called Phillip at the office, and we went to look at the house. Phillip made an offer as we walked down the front stone steps. Phillip was a senior partner, Jimmy Carter was president, the interest rate was at eighteen percent, and we got a steal.

I waited for Friday when Phillip took the 5:10 instead of the 7:10 and was on his second drink to tell him we should move to the city.

"Listen, let me go over this again with you. We got this house. I told you then it was for midgets, but you insisted, so we bought it. Then you wanted something bigger. You kept badgering me. Now we find a house I like. The property is great. And wasn't it you who said yes when I asked if we should put an offer in on it?"

"I wasn't thinking."

"Well, too bad. They've accepted it."

"People change their minds."

"We're not."

"Can't we make it lighter?"

"Will you let me take a breath?"

We sold the small house to a couple with twin daughters, and a local moving company, the Harvey Brothers, moved us to Sheppard Road the day after Thanksgiving.

The house was built in 1907 as a summer cottage for an admiral. There was a large ship's bell by the front door, and the end of the dining room, with its eight curved windows, resembled the bow of a ship. It stood on three acres and had fourteen rooms and four fireplaces. I wondered what made the admiral plant pines around a house in the middle of an apple orchard. I told Phillip we should have them cut down.

"The pines protect the house," he said.

"How do they protect the house? If anything, the house will be destroyed if one of them falls."

"The pines can be seen from town."

"Phillip, they're not pretty trees."

"We are not cutting down hundred-year-old pines."

Carole and George

My mother always hung the sheets out in the sun to dry. Every morning, if it wasn't raining or snowing, the bedding would air on the sill of an open window.

I asked Phillip if he would string a clothesline between the apple tree and the pine closest to the house. Phillip told me to have Michael do it. No matter how tight Michael and I tied the end of the forty-foot cotton line around the trunk of the pine, it sagged in the middle. I asked Michael if we should give up and buy an unfolding type, and he asked when I was taking him to Action Joe's like I promised.

The next morning I saw a man in a baseball hat pushing a Y-shaped stick into the ground at the middle of the clothesline, lifting it. As I approached, he said in a loud voice, "People around here don't like people who hang their clothes outside. It shrinks up the value of their property."

I laughed. "What a nice thing to do. Thank you."

"I happen to like scotch. Johnnie Walker, if I can get it." He took off his hat and wiped his face against his sleeve. He was going bald.

"I keep a bottle of Black Label under the sink."

"Hey, you're my kind of woman. You can't wrap the line around the tree like that, it won't hold. You need a hook. I think I've got a big one around somewhere." His voice was gruff, but the face was round, pleasant. A folded knife hung by a short piece of nautical rope from his belt. He extended his hand, "George. I'm married to a 'Martha' next door."

I laughed and took his hand. "Amine."

"What kind of name is that?"

"It's Arabic."

"No kidding. You don't look foreign. Anyway, welcome to the pretense."

"It is, isn't it? Why do you think it's like that?"

"Who the hell knows? Maybe it's the water."

"Would you and your wife like to come over for dinner?"

"Sure. It'll be nice to get a home-cooked meal."

I made a fire in the dining room, and by the time George and his wife Carole walked over, the chill was gone. The room needed just a few candles lit.

Carole was tall, almost as tall as George. She wore a green wool crepe pantsuit, and her curly blond hair was tied back in an orange and yellow polka-dot bow. She brought over an antique crock tied in a wide, pink silk ribbon and filled with unshelled peanuts.

"You have two little girls, I saw them playing outside. There's enough ribbon for both of them. You can't get ribbon like this anymore; I got a whole roll of it at an estate sale in Irvington. My daughter Eloise can baby-sit for you. You have a boy too, right? He must be, what? Eight? You really have young kids. Jesus, thank god mine can be on their own now."

"When was it any different?" said George.

"When's your furniture coming?" Carole bit into her lower lip.

"It's here," I said.

"Hey, Carole, it's a lot better than the garage sale we have next door."

"You haven't been inside a furniture store your whole life, so why don't you just shut up?"

We sat down to dinner.

"Phillip, that's a nice Porsche you have out there. How about letting me drive it sometime?"

Before Phillip's eyes could lift up from his steak, I said, "Sure, George."

Phillip went upstairs before dessert, and George left soon after. Carole stayed, and we talked till two.

Lorritta

Ted owned the High Yield Pet Shoppe in Katonah, he used to be a commodities broker. Phillip took the children there on the Saturdays he didn't work. He bought a saltwater tank and tropical fish. Ted told him the kids would love watching a lobster shed its skin, and Phillip bought one. He returned the lobster after Charlotte saw it eat her angelfish and in exchange he got a huge brown rabbit he named Rex.

Phillip bought an Amazon lilac crown parrot for Michael's ninth birthday. Ted told Phillip it was hard to know the sex or age of parrots, but he had a feeling she was young. He also told Phillip she'd talk a lot, that Lorritta means "little parrot" in Spanish, and that it had probably been said to her over and over on the boat bringing her from South America.

Phillip paid five hundred dollars for her. He also bought her a large cage, a mirrored ball that hung by a thin chain from one of the bars, powdered vitamins to mix with her seed, and absorbent cedar flakes for the bottom of her cage.

There's a home movie of Michael standing by Lorritta's cage trying to make her say something other than "Lorritta." But with all the coaxing, she will only say her name. If someone laughs, she'll answer with a laugh uncannily the same. If there's more than one person laughing, her laugh becomes unrecognizable.

She likes it when I put her on my shoulder; she'll bend her head down against my cheek, and I'll rub the spot where her feathers separate.

On warm days I would bring her in her cage out on the lawn and spray her with water. She would spread her wings, and we'd laugh, and after she dried out in the sun, I'd move her in her cage to the shade.

One warm, late autumn afternoon, I saw her from the kitchen window standing on top of her cage. I walked slowly toward her, and she flew up into one of the pines. I called her, and she laughed.

I phoned Ted. "Put what she likes in her cage. I remember she liked peanut butter. Be sure to put it where she can see it. She'll come down."

Katherine and Charlotte made a long line of graham crackers spread with peanut butter from the pine to the cage and kept calling her. I didn't see Michael. I found him in his room sitting in a corner, his arms around his knees, his head down, sobbing.

"Michael? Sweetie. What?"

"Pop's going to yell at me."

"Why would Pop yell at you?"

"She's my bird and I didn't take care of her."

"Darling, it's not your fault. Lorritta just got out of her cage. That's all. She'll come back."

I couldn't get Michael to come out of his room. I was outside to meet Phillip when he came up the drive that evening.

"What happened?"

"Nothing happened. Everything's fine."

"Who's hurt?"

"Nobody's hurt."

"Then why are you out here?"

"Lorritta got out of her cage."

"Okay, so put her back in."

"She's in one of the pines."

"Goddamn it Amine, I knew this was going to happen."

"Phillip, it's no big deal."

"Where's Michael?"

"Phillip. Michael's very upset."

"He should be. That bird was his responsibility."

"Phillip. Please. He's upset enough. And why are you talking about Lorritta in the past tense?"

"He's in his room?" I let Phillip walk past me, up the front stone steps, and into the house.

Michael's room was above the kitchen, and I heard Phillip yelling at him.

They came down the back staircase. Phillip told Michael to turn on the outside lights. Through the window I watched Michael stop at Lorritta's cage. Phillip walked on toward the pine looking up into its dark branches. Katherine and Charlotte quietly played in their rooms.

I found Ted's home number in the phone book.

"Don't be upset, Mrs. Calt. She'll come down. They live in trees. Guaranteed she'll be in her cage tomorrow morning. They get hungry after a while."

In the early morning I went out, and I heard her in the pine by the garage.

"You better get someone over here." And Phillip left for work.

When the children got up, we stood under the pine, looking into the dense branches; Lorritta was green, and it was hard to see if she was still there. She answered when we called. Happy that she was still there, the children got dressed. I gave them breakfast and drove them to school, stopping at the convenience store, surprising them with Twinkies.

Ted told me there was a tree man in Larchmont. "He's great. I've seen him work. Big guy, but he moves fast."

The man arrived that night with his wife and young son. They wouldn't come in for coffee or tea or milk or chocolate milk or juice or fruit or anything.

"Seeing how it's raining and they're saying the temperature's gonna drop hard, I better get up there." He strapped a wide leather belt around his waist and started to climb the hundred-foot pine. His wife and son stood by their car in the heavy rain. She held a flashlight and beamed it just ahead of her husband. We stood under an eave of the house, sheltered from the downpour.

He came down about twenty minutes later. "I'm sorry. I was like five feet from her, and she took off. Goddamn, I'm sorry." He took off his belt, threw it into the back of the station wagon, and got in. He rolled down his window and told Phillip not to bother paying him and drove down the drive with his wife beside him and their son in her lap.

I waited for Phillip to turn off the light on his side of the bed before asking if Loritta would survive.

"No."

"You shouldn't be angry at Michael. Lorritta flying away is not his fault."

"Amine, you coddle him. He's got to be taught responsibility. When Lorritta was outside, he should have checked the cage to be sure it was secure. He didn't do it, did he? Now the bird is dead, and we all have to suffer because he didn't do his job."

"I was the one who brought Lorritta out. He was in school."

"I am not going to repeat what I said."

After Phillip went to work and before I woke the children, I stood on the lawn and called her. She answered from the other side of the stone wall by the road. The maple had lost most of its leaves during the rainstorm, and I saw her on a high branch through the early morning mist.

I called a tree company. We stood on the stone wall, talking to Lorritta and waiting for the bucket truck to come. When one of the men asked if I had something to lure the bird with, I remembered the doughnuts my mother had made. She left a bag of them in the freezer before she flew back to California.

The man put one of them on the end of a stick, and when Lorritta went for it, he grabbed her.

I put her back in her cage and turned the oven on, leaving the door open to help dry her.

Michael told me he still wanted to go to school. Katherine and Charlotte begged to stay in the kitchen with Lorritta. I listened to their protests all the way to Greenwich.

"You see, Michael, Lorritta didn't want to fly away. Do you see how she stayed close to home? She wanted to come down. She naturally flapped her wings, but that just made her go higher into the pines. But she never left. Do you see how she stayed? Your father didn't mean to yell at you, Michael. He was just afraid of losing her. That's all."

Perched

We rented a house on Nantucket for the month of August. The ad said it was a historic home overlooking a duck pond. My mother asked if she could come. Mrs. Chase, who she cooked for, was going to start spending the summers with her younger daughter in Wisconsin.

The house was on the main road to town, and the duck pond was across the road hidden behind marsh grass. The neighboring houses were rented to college students who worked during the day and partied at night. My mother asked, who rents a house before seeing it?

Phillip taught me to play tennis. We'd leave early in the morning before anyone was up. When we got back, my mother had breakfast waiting for us, and lunch was packed. We went to a beach with no waves and took turns swimming with the children. Phillip taught Michael to ride a bicycle. My mother bought Katherine and Charlotte identical sundresses and tied ribbons in their hair. They walked on either side of their grandmother, holding her hands, when she took them into town. She told them not to pay attention to the people who stared at them. Girls should never show they know they're pretty—being pretty isn't everything.

A complicated deal came in needing Phillip's attention. After he left, my mother told me he was drinking too much, and I was not to allow Michael and Katherine to go to the refrigerator and grab whatever they wanted, whenever they wanted—she couldn't tolerate the lax atmosphere. She told me to drive her to the airport, and she flew back to Los Angeles. The children and I stayed for the remaining two weeks.

I called my mother when we got back to Westchester. We pretended she hadn't left abruptly. I told her Phillip was very busy at work and didn't have time to drink, and we'd bought another dog we named Ret, to keep Bridges active, and she told me I was crazy.

Phillip bought Katherine two bunnies and Charlotte two lovebirds from Ted's. Katherine named her bunnies Black Cloud and White Cloud, and she kept them in her bedroom in a large basket. Charlotte named her birds Peaches and Cream and let them out of their cage at night, and I would find them perched on the bedpost closest to her face in the mornings. We took in a stray cat Katherine named Scratchy. Rex, the rabbit, was kept in a wooden cage by the side of the garage. Another lobster ate all the fish one night. I disconnected the filter from the fish tank and drove the lobster to Rye and let it out in Long Island Sound. Michael ignored Lorritta.

We rented a different house on Nantucket the following summer. My mother went to France and then to Wisconsin for Mrs. Chase's daughter's fourth wedding and arrived in Nantucket a week after we did.

"They had it catered. Awful. I can't understand how people are in business. I made breakfast for them, and they told me I should have done the wedding. I wore my beige knitted suit and the scarf you gave me. How I love that scarf. I tied it around my head." She cracked another egg into the batter. She was making a pound cake. "They say the French are miserable. I don't have a problem with them. Why? Because they don't have patience with people who don't know how to live? I was sitting near four Americans in a café by the Seine, near the Louvre. Two brothers and their wives, or maybe she was a girlfriend, she was Oriental, she was small, but the other three were fat, much bigger than you, and they were drinking Coke from straws, large glasses. Horrible. Filled with ice. That's why there's so much stomach cancer here. The little woman was drinking water. They must keep the straws hidden away and bring them out especially for the Americans."

"You talked to them?"

"About what?"

"How did you know they were brothers?"

"Oh, Amine, come on. I thought about you. You have got to lose weight."

"Mom, do you know you put in fourteen eggs?"

"It's better. If the yolk isn't firm, it means it's not fresh. Give it to the dogs. I was at the open market in Cannes. Fresh food? There was this elegant woman. She showed me how she tied her scarf. It was just right. I was tan. Amine, I don't know what it is. Is the sun different? Is it the air? They tan differently in France. It's not the creams, I use the same creams, and I buy them there. The creams are not the same here. They put something in them here to make them last longer. Why can't they leave everything alone? I bought a new scarf, and I tied it, I looked..." And she looked away. She would never finish such a sentence.

Forget-Me-Nots

Two couples bought three acres on Nantucket with the intention of building their houses on the land. When it was discovered, only after one of the couples had nearly completed building their house, that the land could not be subdivided, the couples stopped being friendly and the unfinished house went into foreclosure.

We bought the house and hired a local carpenter to sheet rock and install pine floors.

Phillip chartered a plane to Nantucket to make sure that the money he gave the carpenter for the materials was used for that purpose. The pilot waited at the airport with the plane while Phillip took a cab to the house and when he saw that the sheet rock and the planks of pine were there, the pilot flew him back to Westchester.

I told the carpenter's friend that before painting the new pine trim around the doors, he should shellac the knots to prevent them from bleeding through. When all the work on the house was completed, and the antique pine furniture Carole had helped me pick out was delivered, I woke up in the early morning sunshine to notice that the knots on all the furniture were shellacked too. When Phillip called that night I told him and we just laughed.

I was pregnant with Stephen. I found a doctor in Westchester who would deliver the baby in a darkened room, cut the umbilical after it had stopped pulsating, and quietly lay the baby in a basin of warm water. Music would play; I chose Mozart. On my due date, the doctor's nurse called and asked me to come in to take a stress test. The doctor examined me, looked at my chart, and said there had been a mistake, it would be another three weeks before I gave birth. My mother took the children to Nantucket. Why should everyone be in Westchester waiting another three weeks when they could be on the beach? My eyes filled with tears as Phillip drove the station wagon down the drive a few days later. The children were nodding off, and my mother, sitting next to Phillip, waved good-bye.

I woke up in the morning to let the dogs out and remembered they weren't there. No one was. They were all on Nantucket, and I was alone waiting for my baby to be born.

My mother would answer the phone and tell me the children were behaving and listening to her. Katherine told me she and Charlotte watched *The Young and the Restless* and Michael got a BB gun and Baba was knitting red sweaters for the bunnies.

Phillip came back to wait with me. He told me my mother was doing a great job with the kids. He left early for work, and I was asleep when he came back.

The doctor reminded me a week before I was due not to eat anything after six at night. I didn't listen and ate three large California nectarines and felt uncomfortable a few hours later. Phillip drove us to the hospital.

The doctor told me to get off the gurney and onto the delivery table just as my body went into a spasm.

"Get ahold of yourself. I need you on the table, now."

I moved and involuntarily pushed. The baby came out along

with the nectarines. The doctor jumped back, and the nurse caught Stephen.

Stephen was three days old when he and I flew to Nantucket. Phillip left on an earlier flight; we never flew together. I nursed Stephen as the plane overshot the runway twice because of the fog.

Carole met us at the airport. Their house on Pineapple Street has been on George's side of the family since the 1890s.

"He looks exactly like Charlotte. Let me hold him." She reached to take him. "Amine, I better get you home. You don't look good."

The children and my mother were waiting for us in the driveway. She took Stephen from me and told Carole it would be better if she left—"Amine needs to be in bed."

The house smelled of dill and chicken soup. "I asked your husband to get me some organic chickens. He had them flown in. That's what I call a man."

The children picked flowers from the garden and put them in Ball jars and placed them on every table and windowsill.

"Aminachka, he looks like you. I'll take him upstairs. You go take a bath."

In a wicker basket were three down pillows, each one encased in a white linen sham of sparsely scattered forget-me-nots. It stood on the rag rug beside Phillip's and my bed. I went into the bathroom where my mother had also prepared a bath for me.

Charlotte came into the bedroom, pretending she hadn't heard her grandmother tell her not to go upstairs. She climbed into bed with me, put her face on top of mine, and told me how much she loved me. She looked down on Stephen sleeping in his basket and told him she loved him too. She started jumping up and down on the bed, singing his name, and then falling on him as my mother came into the room with a tray of soup and tea.

In one motion, Charlotte was lifted off of Stephen and the tray was on the dresser. My mother then screamed at Charlotte to get out of the room and collapsed into the wicker rocking chair. The kitchen towel over her left shoulder fell to the floor.

I heard Phillip come in. At the airport they told me his plane had been rerouted to Hyannis. When he heard the scream, he ran upstairs, immediately sized up the situation, swung Charlotte out of our room into hers, and ran back.

"Phillip, you have to do something. This cannot go on. They're going to kill him. She doesn't care. There has to be discipline in this house."

I got out of bed and walked into the room Charlotte shared with her sister. I lay next to her and began kissing her wet cheeks, nose, eyes, telling her what a funny story she will be able to tell Stephen when he grows up and how he'll laugh and laugh and laugh.

"Leave her alone. She should be punished. It's the baby who needs you. Can't you hear him crying?" I couldn't tell if it was Phillip's voice or my mother's.

The Cold War

I first met Nina in Moscow. Sarah introduced us at the film festival. Nina was tall, too tall, she said, to continue pursuing ballet. I couldn't help glancing at her high heels. She laughed. "I don't care." Her blond hair was pulled back, tied in a knot, and lay at the nape of her neck. She wore a purple dress, a large fringed shawl with red and green poppies thrown over her left shoulder. We talked about the director of the film she produced and the face creams she buys only in Paris. She asked if Sarah and I would like to have dinner with her and her husband, Serge, the following evening.

For a few days, toward the end of June, Moscow's air is filled with small, floating white fluffs from its poplar trees. As they settle to the ground, they're gathered into small piles and burned. An old woman with a broom told Sarah and me that we had just passed building number four, and she pointed to an ornate yellow archway across the street. The foyer smelled of urine, earth, and wet cement. A wide marble staircase circled the elevator, which wasn't working. As we climbed the stairs, Sarah noticed the handrail was missing. We moved closer to the stairwell wall and tried not to look down.

Nina greeted us at her door. "I'm sorry there's no electricity. They cut the cable. By mistake, of course. Just now the generator came on. Imbeciles. I am so happy you are here. I said to Serge, finally, women who don't want anything from me."

Her toenails were painted red. Sarah and I took off our shoes and placed them next to a Chinese urn filled with umbrellas.

Nina told us nine families had occupied the apartment and that it took a year to get them out and another year to bring it back to the way it once was. "It is inhuman to live in a communal apartment." Wall sconces, oriental carpets, leather couches, chairs, ottomans, and Italian laminated furniture filled the rooms.

Serge arrived a few minutes later. He was a large man with light eyes, and his brown wavy hair fell to his shoulders. He looked younger than Nina. He wore jeans, an open-collared shirt, and sandals. He kissed Nina on the lips, bowed to Sarah and me, and went to the kitchen to make a few phone calls.

Sarah and I sat with Nina in the living room, eating beluga caviar, drinking ice-cold vodka, discussing films, and listening to Artur Rubinstein play Chopin mazurkas.

Serge came in and sat next to me. I felt his unease, and I stopped leaning against the soft cushion of the couch and listened intently to his view of the current situation in Russia. He said he could live anywhere in the world, and he would live nowhere else but in Moscow. "It's like your Wild West, when everything was possible. But, now Moscow and our apartment are quiet. Nina's son is with his grandmother at my dacha."

Serge asked if we would like to hear Elton John. Nina smiled. I thought he'd put on a CD. Instead, he got up and told us we'd have to leave right now. Elton John was performing for only one night at the Kremlin, and even though it was a few blocks away, it would be faster if his chauffeur drove us.

He told us to stay close to the stairwell wall going down, that he was replacing the elevator with one from England. Duplicates in titanium of the iron handrail and spindles were being hand-turned in Italy and would be arriving in a day or so. The building was his. He planned to sell each floor for three or four million. He'd have the best security system, the wires would be hidden in the walls. Nina, Sarah, and I followed the beam of his flashlight down the eight flights of stairs.

We walked on broken concrete to the waiting white BMW with dark windows, and we drove past the old woman slowly sweeping. It took us half an hour to get within a block of Red Square. Serge told us we would have to walk the rest of the way. The concert crowd got larger as we made our way to the bridge leading to the Kremlin. The women stood straight, sculptured in their tight dresses. The precious stones on their necks, wrists, and fingers matched the color of their clutched purses. The men, shorter, older, rounder, in double-breasted suits, held the bent elbows of their women. We passed uniformed security guards, and I breathed in the changing scent of French perfume.

Serge bought tickets from a scalper. The four of us were scattered among the first two rows of the theater. The man next to me said these seats cost at least a thousand dollars if bought that night. A sociologist whom Sarah and I met earlier that week outside the one remaining synagogue in Moscow told us Russia was rich, it didn't matter how many times she was robbed, she still could give more. It was a great concert. Sarah and I were the only ones clapping and swaying to the music. Everyone else sat silently in their seats.

We insisted on taking a cab back to the apartment where we were staying. Serge held me deep under my arm, and I felt his breath on my cheek as he guided me in to the backseat. Nina gave the driver twenty dollars before Sarah and I could stop her.

A year went by, and in the middle of that summer Nina called. She and Serge had arrived in New York the previous afternoon.

They had called Sarah. Her answering machine said she was in California.

I met them at the Carlyle, and we had lunch at an outdoor café. They were on their way to Niagara Falls. They would be back in a week, spend a night, and fly out the following evening for Milan to buy clothes for the fall.

"Is Westchester near Niagara Falls?"

"No. But it's on the way. Why don't you spend the night with us?"

I told Phillip they were coming. "They'll only be here one night."

"You know I hate Russians."

"Serge and Nina took Sarah and me out, and they spent a lot of money on us, and I want to thank them. Please."

"Fine."

They arrived a week later, in a rented car. They had enjoyed Niagara Falls, but somehow they had expected more.

Serge asked if there was a computer store nearby; he wanted to buy a laptop and the new Windows program. I drove them to White Plains, and while he was in the store, Nina and I went for coffee. She told me it was always wonderful being with Serge alone. In Moscow there were too many distractions. She needed to buy her son a schoolbag, nothing expensive, he was only seventeen. She didn't buy anything for Serge's daughter. "She gets enough from her father."

For dinner I cooked steaks and corn on a mesquite fire, prepared a salad from the garden, baked brownies, and made lemon sorbet in the machine I'd received as a gift from the children on Mother's Day.

Phillip came home from work, and we had drinks by the pool. The mosquitoes forced us to eat in the dining room. I had forgotten to replenish the citronella candles. The children were away; Michael was in California at a bike race, Katherine and Charlotte were in Chile skiing, and Stephen was in a cabin with ten other twelve-year-old boys near the top of Mount Washington. Phillip excused himself before dessert, telling Serge he knew nothing about computers but that his secretary had one.

"Is he always like this?"

"He works very hard, and he has to get up early."

Serge and Nina slept in the guest room. A small pitcher in a Nantucket basket, holding snapdragons and roses from the garden, stood on a table by their bed next to *Computers Today* and *Vogue*.

They were up at eleven. Serge wanted to go back to the computer store before driving to the airport. I had breakfast waiting for them: cantaloupe with blueberries; a feta cheese, tomato, and spinach omelette; toasted peasant bread with butter I had made from organic heavy cream; and beach plums preserved the previous fall. Coffee with steamed milk.

"Phillip has left?"

"He took an early train to work this morning."

"He's a quiet man. Interesting."

I waved to them as they drove down the drive.

After clearing breakfast, I went upstairs to take the sheets off the bed. Nina's black silk nightgown lay under a pillow. I decided not to mail it. I heard that nothing anyone sends to Russia is received.

Two years later Nina called.

"I am in New York. Sarah gave me your new number. Why is it unlisted? She told me you had been living in New York and that you moved back to Westchester. Is that true? Why?"

"It's a long story."

She told me she was going on a Caribbean cruise and had brought nothing with her. She needed to go shopping, and where could she go? She told me she didn't know what to buy. "Isn't the weather in the Caribbean warm? Aren't the nights cool? I've brought nothing with me. I should have at least brought a coat that I could wear at night, on deck. Would a fur be too hot? What should I do?"

I asked her about Serge. She told me she was too upset to talk about him. All she wanted to do was think about clothes. She didn't want to cry. She was leaving tomorrow. She would go to Saks now and buy whatever else she needed on the boat even though it would be more expensive. "I don't care. I will be back in three weeks. I will call you, and we will see each other. Please, I have to see you."

"I have the black nightgown that you left."

"Keep it. I do not wear black anymore. I will call you. Please be home."

She called three weeks later, at night. She told me she'd been back for two days, either sitting in her hotel room or walking the streets. She didn't buy anything, didn't even look, she just walked. I asked her when she was leaving for Moscow. Her voice rose slightly. "Tomorrow, at three, my plane is leaving."

I told her I'd meet her at her hotel in an hour.

"Are you sure? Is it too late? I know you get up early. I will be waiting for you. Thank you."

It took me close to two hours to drive in. Her hotel was on Forty-Eighth Street off Broadway, and I had forgotten about the theater crowds.

Through the revolving glass door of the hotel, I saw her. She was dressed in white, and she stood by the newspaper stand in the narrow lobby. Her hair looked dull, and she was too tan. Seeing me, she waved. We embraced, and she held on to me. Taking me by my arm, she said, "Let's go have a drink."

We sat at the far corner of the hotel bar. She had a Murphy's

Red, I had a Beck's Dark. The man sitting next to her lit her long, thin cigarette.

"It's so good to see you," she said. "I missed not speaking Russian."

"Did you have a good time?"

"Yes, it was truly wonderful. Serge had offered me a world cruise before, and I told him no. I thought, how can I be on a boat for months? If I had known what it was like, I would have gone. Amine, it was wonderful. It was like a movie. The people were older, of course, mostly couples. We would all get dressed for dinner. I wore my hair down. I bought a moisturizer with a slight tint to it so I didn't have to wear makeup. I only did my eyes. I wore very short dresses. I look tired now, I know, but then I wasn't. I slept to eleven. Oh Amine, it was great. Dancing. I danced with this man, and when I sat down, this woman next to me whispered, 'Do you know who you were dancing with?' No, I said, who? She said, 'A famous actor.' And I said, who? She said he was very famous, but she couldn't remember his name and I didn't know who he was. He and I spent the entire evening together. You know, he touched my hair and my ear, and we talked politics. He said, 'You know, Nina, I like you, and I would invite you to my cabin but I have too much respect for you.' Amine, it was wonderful. It was a Norwegian ship. All the staff, they were all so tall and in these wonderful white uniforms, looking so elegant. The first few nights I sat at a table with very nice people. Our server quietly said to me, 'Nina, tomorrow night you sit at another table.' I said no, I like this one. He said, 'No, you listen to me. You sit at another table.' And I do, and I meet this wonderful couple from Ohio. What is the city in Ohio?"

"Columbus?"

"Yes, Columbus, Ohio. Amine, they were wonderful. He is an orthopedist, and they told me they have two men for me. One is a lawyer, and the other one is a doctor. I will visit them in July."

"Tell me about you and Serge."

"I told you, I don't want to think about it. It just gets me upset. How's everything with you?"

"I want to leave Phillip."

"Why?"

"Why? When you were talking about dancing, I thought, Phillip wouldn't dance with me. I'd ask him, and he'd say, 'You know I hate to dance.' We danced, once, at a Christmas party. There was a game, a hat gets passed around, music plays. When the music stops, the man left with the hat leaves the dance floor with his partner, they're eliminated. Phillip danced with me as if I was a rag doll. We won a bottle of champagne, and I don't remember if we drank it together."

"So? Amine, does he want this?"

"No."

"Do you know what you're doing? He's a very successful man. And like all successful men, very complicated."

"Um."

"How old are you?"

"I'll be fifty-two in May."

"You're older than I am. Do you know how many women, younger than you, would love to have him?"

"I'm sure there are."

"You don't care? Believe me, as soon as he finds someone younger, you will not know what to do with yourself. Do you have someone else?"

"No."

"Amine, you never leave a man unless you have someone better to go to. You will be alone."

"I am alone."

"Amine? What fantasy are you in? You have never been alone. You do not know what being alone is. What do you have to do? Smile when he comes home and go to bed with him? From what I saw, he leaves you alone. He let you go to Russia by yourself. I am talking to you from my heart and as a friend. I like you. You have a man. That is what is important. Everything else is nothing. You do not go anywhere. Whatever you do, you do. Children want their parents together, no matter how miserable it is. Do you think Serge was ever a father to my son?"

"I want to be happy."

"Amine? How naïve you are. You are talking like a child. Life is not about happiness. You cannot do it on your own. A man must do it for you. Especially a woman like you. What life do you have left? There's more behind you than ahead of you. The best years have gone. I am your friend. And you listen to me, hard. You think people will be interested in you? Our friends are now only Serge's friends. That is the way it is. No one wants a middle-aged extra woman. I was the one who was wealthy when we met, Serge was the one who was struggling. My first husband had a lot of money. Of course, not like the money Serge has now. Serge told me he made his first million five years ago. How much he has now, I will never know. I told him the law is half. He laughed. He has it all hidden, Switzerland, New Zealand. Get anything? I cannot even prove there is anything. I only get what he decides to give me, and as the months go by, he forgets what I was to him, and I get less and less. Why did I not go on the world cruise when he offered it to me? I will not be dumb again. He wanted to take me to Cartier's the last time we were here. I said to him, no, why now? Later. Now I cannot find him even when I want him. I had everything. Four furs, two hundred pairs of shoes. Now everything is old, and I want it all new. It is terrible. I do not want to talk about it anymore. He gave me the apartment. I have to live somewhere. You know, I built the apartment myself, with what strength. Everything was a major crisis. It is not like here, where you pick up the phone and you have your choice of everything and everything is delivered to you. There? I went all over Moscow for everything. Everything I wanted was imported, and you had to know where to find it, and the location changed every day, sometimes twice in one day. And he told me I do not do anything. Everything you do is forgotten. Stay, and if you need another life, have it, but do not leave. I go back tomorrow, and I do not know what there is for me there. I called my son last night, and he told me he misses me. I am going to Ohio in July, and on the way back I will see you."

"You're a producer."

"Producer? Of what? Are you in this world? Amine, there is no film industry left in Russia. Did I get paid for that film? I paid to have that film made, and now my bank is gone. Why is that man staring at me? He cannot understand I am not interested in him? We are alike, Amine, you and I. It takes us a long time to want a man. I think I am going to have Serge send me to a spa in Italy. I need rest. Amine, dye your hair. You have a young face, why age yourself with hair that has no color? Amine, you stay. You have no good reason. Be a free woman and stay."

I told her it was late and I had to get up early.

She told me she'd walk with me to the car.

As we stood up to leave, the slight man sitting next to Nina asked if it was Russian we were speaking. I said yes, Nina said no.

The man looked at Nina and asked, "Why is your friend saying yes and you're saying no?"

"I do not like you," Nina said as she walked to the door of the bar. The man smiled and then shrugged. I followed her out.

She put her arm through mine as we walked along Broadway to the garage. I drove her back to her hotel. She leaned over and kissed me and said she'd call me from Moscow. "Thank you for coming. You know I am frightened. I will come in July, and we will go shopping."

Fresh Fruit

Nadya, Elena, and I sat in the living room eating a seven-layer chocolate cake and drinking tea. Nadya had a doctorate in Russian literature and had taught at the university in St. Petersburg. Elena was a biologist and was also from St. Petersburg. Elena brought photographs she took at the Halloween party we went to.

I met them at an art exhibition, they knew the painter. They worked as housekeepers for a family who owned a townhouse on Riverside Drive and an estate in South Salem. The family's wealth came from Siberian gas.

It was an overcast Sunday afternoon in late November. I started a fire in the fireplace using twigs I had gathered on a walk through Central Park that morning. Phillip had taken Stephen to a soccer tournament in Brewster. Charlotte was in her room sleeping. Katherine was training in Colorado with the Dartmouth ski team. Michael was at a cycling race in North Carolina.

"A friend of mine in Peter's married a man thirty years younger. I just got a letter from her. Before they married, they lived together for thirteen years. She's sixty and he's thirty now. She was his teacher. She's a brilliant woman and very charming. He was eighteen, and she was forty-eight and married. She was eight years older than her first husband, fifteen years older than her second husband. When they first met, I told her to stay away from Victor; she would ruin his life; she wouldn't be able to give him children. She told me he doesn't go away. She's tried. He insisted and insisted. Finally, she left her husband, who was this tall, handsome Georgian. A real man. She had a son with him; the boy stayed with his father. Victor did everything for her; she remained his teacher. She had a sick mother who lived on the outskirts of Peter's. Victor would take a couple of buses there to bring her food and news of her daughter. The mother thought nothing of him, just another student twirling around her daughter. Through my friend's connections he moved ahead in his life. His parents were construction workers, and in the social order of things, that is the lowest a person could be. She helped him, and he became very successful in business. He's clean, he's not involved in anything dirty. He's not a crook. Now he's bought her son, who's married, an apartment for him and his wife. Her mother lives with them now. She complains to me, 'Oh he is so dumb.' But I tell her, 'Anastasia Sergevena, Victor is very good to you. He buys you fruit and you like fruit. Who can now afford fresh fruit?' My friend thought she could discourage him by showing him how unattractive she can be. She went under the shower, she has a narrow forehead, but she makes it as least noticeable as she can. But with her hair slicked back, you can see how narrow it is. She has a large nose and she has enormous breasts, like watermelons, DDDD. They go down to her waist. She calls him in, and he looks at her and he says, 'Oh, my beauty. I love you.'" We laughed.

"What do you do?" Nadya said. "He loves her. She doesn't have to say a thing, it's done. He bought her a sable coat for her sixtieth birthday, and he brought home sixty roses. She said their perfume alone was . . . They recently got married. Not in the registry office but in church, which is much more serious. So you see?"

You Can Be Sure

We bought a house in Bedford as an investment. Its appreciation through the years would pay for our children's college education.

We bought the house from Mrs. Keenan. Her husband had died of heart failure a week after they moved in, leaving her alone to raise their six sons.

She and I sat in the kitchen having tea while the engineer we hired went through the house, noting things that needed to be fixed on a yellow legal pad. She told me she was a nurse and worked the eleven P.M. to seven A.M. shift at Good Samaritan Hospital. "I've been doing it so long, the hours don't bother me anymore." Her boys were a handful, there wasn't a weekend night she didn't get a call at work from the police telling her one of them was caught drinking again. Her youngest was going off to college, and she didn't need a large house anymore. "I'm going to get myself one of those condominiums in Hemlock Farms. A one-bedroom. That's all I need."

We had the eleven rooms painted, the downstairs floors refinished, and the upstairs recarpeted. We rented the house to a divorced surgeon and his two grown sons. After six months they stopped paying rent.

"It's not easy evicting tenants," a litigator told Phillip.

Four months later they were gone. They took their bodybuilding equipment and left five dogs, two of them dead, eight cats, and two ferrets.

Phillip took a day off from work, got the animals in cages, and brought them to the local ASPCA. The department of public works removed the dead dogs. We decided to sell the house, and the real estate agent advised us to renovate it before putting it on the market.

"You have a great investment here. Money you spend on it, you'll double. Guaranteed. It's in a great location. Great family neighborhood. Cyndi Lauper is looking to buy here. And the house is on five acres. Yes, the land in the back may slope down, but I assure you, it's not a problem. Five acres is still five acres. Bedford zoning law allows you one horse per acre. You can have five horses here."

Phillip told me the house was now "my baby" and that he would approve all expenditures.

There were three estimates for the work; Phillip went with the middle bid.

"Mrs. Calt," said the contractor, "you can't get these urine stains out. No amount of sanding will do it. The whole downstairs. Upstairs? It went right through the carpeting. All the floors. In every room. We'll have to re-tile the bathrooms. It's a good thing the floor in the basement is cement. Cement is pretty indestructible. All we need to do with that is wash it down with a strong chemical solution and then paint it. A nice battleship gray should do it."

"Mrs. Calt, since your husband okayed replacing the floor, why don't you suggest knocking out the wall between the kitchen and family room to him? There's a big hole in it anyway. This way you'll get to see a nice fire burning in the fireplace as you're making dinner."

The contractor hired a subcontractor for the kitchen counters and cabinets. The contractor was paid, but instead of paying the subcontractor, the contractor became ill and moved to Florida where bankruptcy laws are lenient.

Phillip hired the contractor who came in with the highest bid.

"Mrs. Calt, did you know that they laid the new flooring over rotted subflooring? There's no way you can save what was put down. Everything will have to be ripped up. If you like, we'll cut it up for you and you can use it for kindling. We'll give you a new subflooring, and we'll use wood that's been kiln dried. This way it won't buckle up at you. We'll lay brand-new oak floors, and you can be sure the job will be done right this time."

The house didn't sell. It was a problem that most of the five acres were unusable. It was advised to landfill the gully, remove the weeping willows, and create an expansive lawn.

During the renovation of Sheppard Road, the doorknobs from all the doors were removed. The doors were stripped of old paint, planed, sanded, primed, and repainted. The doorknobs were placed in two large plastic buckets.

"Mrs. Calt, we can't find the doorknobs. Someone must have taken them, or else they were thrown out by mistake. They're gone. I don't even know where to tell you to get them. They're an odd size. They'd have to be specially made. It'll be expensive, being that they were solid brass and old."

Phillip came home after I finally fell asleep. I knew he'd come home because when I went downstairs, his door was closed. He used one of his black socks to hold it shut: the door that opened to the room that was once ours and was now his.

He began to take care of himself, cycling on weekends, using lite mayonnaise and firming neck cream, having one brimming glass of red wine to help clear his arteries and, to be safe, a small piece of Belgian chocolate. He took vitamins and read Paramahansa Yogananda. Lying in bed after taking a cold shower, a large white towel wrapped around his waist, he exercised his gums with a rubber-tipped metal instrument.

I'll take the dust ruffle. It was ordered from England. It cascades, in folds, to the plum-colored carpet. I'll take it. It'll remove the softness from the bed.

Did Not Finish

Phillip thought the children should learn to ski; the more involved they were in athletics, the better. Skiing was a great family sport, and he wished he knew how when he was young. Phillip was in graduate school when he and a friend went to Sun Valley. His friend told him skiing was easy, and together they rode a chairlift up. His friend took off down a black diamond trail, and left Phillip standing alone. Phillip took off his skis and said he sank to his waist in snow. It took him till nightfall to walk down. He vowed that if he had children, they would know how to ski. He became a managing partner at his firm, his percentage went up, and we bought a townhouse in the White Mountains of New Hampshire.

We drove to New Hampshire every weekend from Thanksgiving to the end of April, after large patches of grass and dirt lay bare and most of the trails were closed. It took five hours to get there, longer if it started to snow on the way. We joined a ski club and enrolled the children in its intensive program. They all became expert skiers, especially Katherine.

There's a picture of Katherine at eight months, sitting against a snowbank near Killington, a pair of skis jammed in the snow beside her. She has on a quilted raspberry-colored snowsuit and a white Angora hat, and she's smiling. She was always fast. She started walking at nine months. She fell against the kitchen table, and her nose wouldn't stop bleeding. I took her to the emergency room, and they told me it should be left alone, that it wasn't as bad as it looked, and that I should just keep her comfortable. In the middle of the night I found Phillip asleep, on the floor, next to her crib.

When she was four, Phillip bought her a dark blue velvet dress with embroidered rosebuds she picked out. She wore that dress over black leotards and tights every day to school.

"Kate, I will not let you wear that dress again. You can't get it off in time to go to the bathroom."

Every morning there would be tears, and she would wear the dress.

I met with the school psychologist.

"Amine, think about it. What's the big deal? So she pees in her pants. She's peeing in her pants, not in yours. Leave it alone. Don't make an issue out of it."

"Katherine, I cannot let you wear that dress again to school. It's difficult for you to take it off, you don't get to the bathroom in time. Take the dress off, and put something else on. I mean it. Do it now."

I went into the basement to put in a load of wash before taking the children to school and saw Katherine sitting midstair, in her leotards, clutching her dress, crying.

"Dolly, do you really want to wear that dress?"

She wore it through the summer into the fall, and when she couldn't get her arms through the sleeves, she let me hang it on a blue velvet hanger in the downstairs closet.

She started ski racing when she was eight.

"That's Katherine Calt coming down. If she doesn't DNF, she'll be in first place."

Each mountain had its top girls, and they'd ski against each other every weekend from January to the end of March. Katherine usually won. Each mountain had its group of fathers standing along the race course or waiting at the finish line. They knew who belonged to whom. They tuned and waxed their daughters' skis, got them to the mountain on time, made sure their equipment was the best: four pairs of skis, two sets of slalom, two for giant slalom, one pair for training, the other for racing, boots sized smaller than her foot so she could feel the snow. Gate-crashing helmets, face guards, gloves, slalom suits, GS suits, poles. No neck or boot warmers—anything extra would slow her down. They checked snow conditions before each race to know which wax to apply. Soft snow, apply a fast wax. If it's icy, get the edges of the skis sharper so she can really cut into it. Apply Cera-F, the miracle wax, just before she takes the chairlift up for her first run. It'll give her an advantage. So what if it costs a hundred and twenty dollars? It should last till she gets to the bottom. They all had their stopwatches and their start order sheets, and they'd note the time it took the top girls to get down. If she placed well, his arm went around her; if she didn't or if she did not finish, they stood apart, she looking down, he looking at the scoreboard.

Greenwich and Florida

The two-thousand-acre farm adjacent to the children's school was being subdivided into large lots. I knew it would be a good investment, and I looked at a fifteen-acre parcel with Mr. Flynn, a former private investigator.

"If I were you," he said, "I'd build right here." We stood on a hill overlooking the wider part of the lake.

"Can you swim in the lake?"

"Would you swim in it?"

"I would if I could. I'd rather swim in a lake than a pool or the ocean, really."

"Ocean scares you."

"Yes."

"The lake water is fed from an underground spring. The water's safe, and it's very clean. You have little kids so you'll probably want to put in a beach."

"No. Actually I wouldn't. I'd like to keep it natural."

"Look." He pointed to an eagle on a high branch of a copper

beech tree. "Watch." He stretched his arms and began making figure eights, slowly, first with one arm, then the other. I held my
breath as the eagle flew within a few feet of us.

He told me the association would protect the land. I wouldn't
have to drive the children to and from school, they could walk.
There were days when I made the trip seven times. My car was
three years old, and it had close to a hundred and fifty thousand
miles on it.

"I hope you buy this land."

"Mr. Flynn, I'd build a square house. The downstairs would be
just this one big room with a lot of windows where you can sit and
watch the sun come up and go down. Wouldn't that be lovely?"

"Yes."

Phillip thought Greenwich was overpriced. He wanted to buy
something in Florida.

On the children's spring break, we drove to Florida and bought
a house on two oceanfront acres from a woman who, after her husband's death, had inherited a cement company, a house in Miami
Beach, and a ranch near what is now Disney World, where, at
eighty-five, she rode a stallion and shot armadillos with her
Winchester. She finished off a fifth of Jack Daniel's every night and
smoked two packs of Marlboros, ripping off the filter of each cigarette. "It's the chemicals they put in these white buggers that kill
you." She wanted to leave Miami because of the Cubans, and she
bought the house on the ocean farther north. She had a heart attack before moving in, and she wouldn't leave her doctor, Enrico
Diaz. "Remember the name. Best goddamn doctor in the world."
She chose us to buy it because we didn't dicker on the price.

It took a local contractor six months to paint the rooms, install
Mexican tile floors, replace the windows, remove the dead palms,
build a new enclosure for the swimming pool, plant a 2,500-square-
foot area with dune grass, connect a lawn sprinkling system, lay new
walkways in mildew-resistant brick, and repave the circular drive.

We flew down to Florida to spend Thanksgiving, and when we left, my father, Rosa, and their friends drove down to stay in the house for the winter.

Natalie called me from Berkeley, where she had decided to stay after college, and told me her life wasn't adding up to very much.

"What do you mean?"

"It's like I'm under water."

"Don't think about it."

Undone

On a warm, sunny afternoon in late November, I picked up Katherine and Charlotte from school and drove them to their riding lesson. Michael was at a soccer game and Stephen was home with a baby-sitter.

Halloween pumpkins still stood at some of the entrances to the estates we passed. The car's radio was on, and Madonna was singing "Like a Virgin." Katherine leaned toward me and asked, "Mommy, what's a virgin?" She was seven, Charlotte was six.

"A virgin, darling, is a girl or a woman who hasn't had a penis in her vagina."

"Mommy, I want to tell you ... Oh, nothing." She leaned back in her seat.

"Tell me what, Dolly?" I slowed the car.

"Babakye ..."

I pulled the car alongside a huge oak.

"Katie, darling, what about Babakye?"

"He puts his finger in my and Charlotte's vagina."

Charlotte sat silent next to her sister.

"Katie, when does he do this?"

"When he and Rosa come over."

"Katie, what does he do?"

"He gives me and Charlotte candy and we sit on the couch."

"And darling, what does he do?"

"He scratches our back and then he puts his finger in our vaginas and we eat candy."

"Katie, darling, where am I?"

"You're in the kitchen with Rosa."

I sat on the split-rail fence watching Katherine and Charlotte's lesson. Their blond ponytails stuck out from under their black velvet hats. Katherine's hair ribbon was about to come undone. They were learning to canter, and they were intently following Mrs. Keel's instructions.

When Phillip came home from work, I told him. Katherine and Charlotte had taken their baths and were quietly playing in their rooms. Michael was doing his homework and Stephen was asleep.

Phillip dialed the number of the Florida house. My father answered, and Phillip asked to speak to Rosa.

"Amine and I just found out that your husband has sexually molested our daughters. This is a despicable way for a grandfather to act. I want you to immediately leave our house. Do you understand? Immediately." He hung up the phone.

"Phillip, please, I want you to go upstairs and let the girls know you know."

He couldn't do it.

I waited a week to call my father in Nyack.

"I want you to stop taking your heart medication, and I want you to go somewhere alone into the woods and die. Because for me you are already dead. And I want you to know that when you die, I will not be at your funeral."

"Amine, what happened? What did I do?"

"You know what you did. I want you to die."

Charlotte wouldn't talk about it. A few weeks went by, and she asked if I loved Babakye. I told her I didn't, that you can only love people who are kind to you, and Babakye wasn't kind.

I went to see a therapist Diana recommended.

"Think about it, Mrs. Calt. Why do you think she asked you that question?"

"Why?"

"She thought if you could stop loving your father, then maybe you could stop loving her. Tell her that it's a firm rule in nature that a parent can never stop loving their child, but a child can stop loving their parent."

I told Charlotte what the therapist told me to tell her.

How I Spent My Summer Vacation

A week before we were to go to Nantucket, Alla, an electrical engineer from Gdansk, who worked as our housekeeper for nearly a year, told me her father suffered a stroke and she had to go back to Poland.

"I know a woman who will help you."

Lillie arrived the next day with a suitcase. When I asked her if she liked it here in America, she answered she was sixty. I later found out she was seventy-eight.

Lillie followed Alla to the attic bedroom to unpack. As I was preparing tea, I heard someone fall down the stairs. When Alla and I lifted Lillie, she screamed. I took her to the emergency room, and she was fitted with a cast that went from her elbow to her wrist.

I hired Carole's sixteen-year-old daughter Eloise to watch the children while I drove Michael to summer camp.

"Mom, just drop me off. I can unpack myself."

I decided not to spend the night at our ski house nearby, and I drove back to Sheppard Road.

We bought a blue Suburban. The salesman convinced Phillip we'd have less glare and more privacy with tinted windows.

I took the third row of seats out and stored them in the garage and started packing the car. I took my six Nantucket baskets that would hang from the beam in the kitchen, ten antique quilts for the beds, four framed, hand-colored photographs by H. Marshall Gardiner, a new lampshade, and a large crock to keep the rabbit food away from the wood rats.

I told Katherine and Charlotte to each pack a bag containing three pairs of underpants, a nightgown, two pairs of shorts, a pair of pants, four T-shirts, a sweater, a pair of sneakers, a pair of sandals, one summer dress, and two bathing suits.

Katherine packed her leotards, ballet shoes, tap shoes, riding boots, and hat, her velvet dress with the lace collar, clothes and hats for her two bunnies, her crystal rabbit collection, her five favorite Madame Alexander dolls, a tablecloth from the linen closet, and dessert napkins from the kitchen drawer for a tea party.

Charlotte packed her Cabbage Patch doll, her complete set of Garbage Pail Kid cards, her ten favorite stuffed animals, the four pillows and the blanket from her bed, her snowball with a little girl, and a lamb she liked to look at while falling asleep, and two Chock-Full-o'-Nuts coffee tins filled with Hello Kitty accessories that had been Eloise's.

I took the dress I was wearing, another dress, a nightgown, and a bathing suit.

Lillie brought whatever she had in her suitcase, and Phillip would bring what he wanted with him when he flew to the island on the weekends.

With bungee cords I secured the children's bicycles to the top of the car's luggage rack. I put Scratchy in his carrier, Lorritta, White Cloud, Black Cloud, Peaches, and Cream in their cages and-piled them one on top of the other in the back-back. I fastened Stephen into his carseat. Lillie sat next to him. Katherine and Charlotte each got a seat by the window, and Bridges and Ret sat in the front with me. I drove down our drive at four in the morning to avoid the traffic on the Connecticut Turnpike and to make it to Hyannis in time for the nine o'clock ferry.

Nantucket is thirty miles off the coast of Cape Cod, and it takes three hours to get there by boat. On board ship Charlotte put the cat in his carrier in the middle of the aisle by our seats. Stephen opened the carrier; Scratchy jumped out; Ret slipped out of his leash and ran after Scratchy; Charlotte and Katherine ran after Ret; Stephen climbed into the cat carrier; Lillie and Bridges slept. I got the children and the animals back in their places and returned to the image I had been having of someone jumping overboard, their body parts in the churning waters of the ship's propeller, and I again forced myself to look calm.

We arrived in the early afternoon. The grass had grown high, the hill was covered in daisies. June rosebuds were climbing up the weathered shingles of the house. The sky was a cloudless blue, seagulls flew in pairs, and the acres of moor were a gentle green. Charlotte and Katherine couldn't wait and climbed out of the open windows of the car. I unlocked the front door with the key that's kept in the right-hand pocket of the yellow slicker hanging in the shed.

It takes two weeks to get the house in order. I wash the floors, walls, windows, doors, screens, bedding, cushions, slipcovers, throw pillows, rag rugs. I bring everything outside, and it's aired by the breeze and warmed by the sun.

I apply butcher's wax to the wide-plank heart pine floor while Lillie sits having tea, the girls tape their legs together with masking tape pretending to be mermaids, and Stephen naps out on the deck under the umbrella.

When he wakes, we'll go to the beach, dinner will have been made, we'll come home, and the children will take their baths. After dinner, I'll read Katherine and Charlotte a book while

Stephen sits in my lap, and before going upstairs I'll make them warm milk with honey. I'll hear Katherine and Charlotte whisper to each other as I'll rock Stephen to sleep. I'll take a bath—a candle will light the windowed room. Phillip will call at nine and tell me he won't be flying in on Friday night. A deal came in, and he'll try for Saturday, late morning, but he won't be able to stay through Monday. He'll have to take the noon plane back on Sunday.

"Did the tree guy come for the Russian olive? It's ridiculous using the wood-burning stove in the summer. But if you insist on doing it, don't let the guy cart the tree away. Tell him to cut the wood in short pieces so they can fit in the stove."

I'll read a book for a while and fall asleep. The house will be quiet. A fire will continue to burn, and the dampness of the night will disappear.

I'll wake up at six to let Scratchy in, let Bridges and Ret out, take the blanket off of Lorritta's cage, and make breakfast. The pot I keep filled with fresh rosemary, lemon rinds, and apple peels will have boiled through the night, and the smell lingers in the morning air.

My mother wanted to see the Florida house, and we planned to meet there in the middle of July. Samantha, who graduated from Hotchkiss with our neighbor's daughter, came to house-sit and take care of the dogs, the cat, and the parrot while the children, Lillie, the bunnies, the lovebirds, and I drove to Florida. I thought at first Lillie could stay, but then I reasoned she didn't drive, she had a broken arm, she didn't speak English, and she needed someone to take care of her.

My mother was flying to Florida from Los Angeles. Mrs. Chase had died, and my mother had been asked to stay on. She turned the lights on in the main house at night and turned them off in the morning. She called whoever was needed for whatever had to be done. She sometimes took care of Mrs. Chase's two grand-daughters when their mother, Jean, went to Santa Barbara to ride.

Natalie was flying in from San Francisco and after two weeks would fly back to continue studying with a Chinese herbalist. My mother would drive back with us to New Hampshire to pick Michael up from camp, and then we'd return to Nantucket.

The Florida house wasn't furnished, and I took eight foam mattresses from the Nantucket attic and attached them to the Suburban's luggage rack with bungee cords. I brought seven sets of sheets, blankets, and pillows, two saucepans, a frying pan, two bowls, cutlery, and dishes for eight. I phoned Rent-All in Florida for a table and eight chairs, as Phillip was planning on flying in for a weekend.

Taking 95 the whole way, the AAA said it could be two days from Nantucket to Florida with an overnight somewhere in North Carolina. There was a steady rain the day we left. I reasoned the mattresses would dry quickly once I took them off and laid them out in the hot Florida sun.

Five miles before reaching the Florida house, we got a flat tire. I left Lillie with the children in the car by the side of the road and hitched a ride with a man in a pickup truck. As the blue Suburban receded in the side-view mirror, I shuddered when I realized I had left an eight-, seven-, and two-year-old with an old woman who didn't speak English and had a broken arm. The man turned his truck around, and I got in the open back with the children. Lillie sat next to the man with her suitcase between them. The man dropped us off at a gas station. We waited for a couple of hours for their tow truck to return so the mechanic could drive us back to the car to fix the tire. He couldn't fix the tire on the road and drove us back to the gas station. The gas station didn't have that size tire, and we waited for a local dealership to deliver a tire that would fit. Phillip said didn't I know that if I had called AAA, the towing wouldn't have cost him anything and where was the spare? I didn't tell him I took it out to make more room in the car.

The house was dirty, and I cleaned it before my mother and Natalie arrived. I washed the floors, windows, bathrooms, kitchen. I bought a tablecloth to hide the stained and chipped rental table. I kept a pot of dried rosemary, lemon rinds, and apple peels boiling on the cooktop to help take the smells out of a house that had been vacated for nine months.

My mother was in agony from the sand fleas that had invaded the mattresses when I left them out on the lawn to dry. She'd go to bed with a long-sleeved shirt, pants, and socks, and she still got up in the night to take a hot shower.

My mother and Lillie didn't get along. "She's going to tell me how to cook?" my mother said to me in Russian, not caring that Lillie understood her. "You couldn't get someone without a broken arm? Or who wasn't ninety? Amine, this is a direct result of your wanting to do everything yourself. You always think you can do it better. Well, here is the result. I will help you with the children and I will cook, but know, I will not clean. I have cleaned enough. If I had cleaned fewer toilets in my life, I would have fewer wrinkles on my face. Learn from me. Don't be a fool."

Phillip flew in and rented a fishing boat for the afternoon. A picture of Stephen holding a two-foot sand shark with his father's help stands framed on my dressing table. That evening I heard my mother say to Phillip I worked too hard, and I heard him reply, "It keeps her humble." And if my mother hadn't laughed, I'm sure she would have slapped him.

My sister and her nieces played on the beach or in the surf. My mother cooked and read Bunin under the palms. Lillie swam in the pool, her cast wrapped in plastic. I took Stephen for walks, and when he went down for his afternoon nap, I took longer and faster walks on the beach, alone.

We spent the night in Savannah and from there drove to New Hampshire, arriving at our ski house at three in the morning. I didn't bother getting anything out of the car. My mother helped me put the children to bed. She and Lillie shared the guest room, and I made my way up the spiral stairs to the master bedroom and fell asleep. I awoke in the dim morning light to a thin layer of red dust over everything: the bedsheets, the rug, the windowsills, the furniture. The management office told me the construction company, dynamiting for the next phase of our development, had accidentally cracked the entry tiles of the houses in our cluster. "They meticulously replaced the damaged tiles. Apparently, when cutting the replacement tiles, the dust became airborne and naturally settled. If you'd chosen a tile that didn't have a color, you probably wouldn't have noticed." My mother went with the children to the Sports Center. Lillie went to pick wildflowers. And I began to clean the house.

The following night, at the camp's closing ceremonies, Michael was awarded top honors in archery, axmanship, canoeing, and survival.

We arrived in Nantucket the next afternoon. The house smelled of dog shit and urine. There was a note on the table, anchored by a seashell, from Samantha: "Sorry I couldn't wait, had to catch the noon ferry. Everybody's fed. Love, Samantha."

I found empty beer cans, wine, and liquor bottles in closets and under the beds, cigarette butts swept into corners, urine stains and dried dog shit on the rag rugs. We couldn't find Scratchy.

My mother went to the beach with the children. Lillie went to pick the Concord grapes she'd seen when we drove up the drive. And I started to clean.

Phillip called to ask me to buy him a pair of Nantucket reds and could I wash the pants and hang them out in the sun to fade? He'd invited the Caseys and their son and daughter for the Labor Day weekend. Could I order lobsters from Manny's before they sell out? Two-pounders for the adults, one-and-a-half for the children, and could my mother make that beet salad and the eggplant caviar? And be sure there's enough to drink, Beth likes Kir Royale, get Taittinger's if Murry's has it, if not, Dom Perignon is fine, and Jim drinks Johnnie Walker Black, and be sure to get plenty of ice and get plenty of hors d'oeuvres. Those smoked oysters were great, and be sure to have plenty of butter and limes, and let's have breakfast at home on Sunday. I'm tired of going out. Can your mother make those Russian pancakes? And get plenty of Canadian bacon and maple syrup. See you Saturday morning.

I took Bridges and Ret to the groomer and had them shaved. I went into town and used the big loaders for the fourteen rag rugs, the slipcovers from the four couches and eight chairs. I washed and waxed the floors. I took the broken screens in so they would be ready by next summer.

An hour after flying in, Phillip went out with Jim, Michael, and James III on the *Outfielder*, the twenty-five-foot Grady White he'd bought after he told me we couldn't afford the nest of antique Nantucket baskets I'd seen in a shop on Main Street. Michael caught a seventy-five-pound yellowfin tuna that he never got to eat because Phillip and Jim gave it to The Woodbox on Fair Street, hoping for a complementary seating for four.

While they were out on the boat, Beth Casey and I went to an auction, where she bought a nautical painting from the 1800s for sixteen thousand dollars. "It's going to look great in our front hall."

My mother made chicken Kiev while Phillip and Jim sat out on the deck and had "a well-deserved drink." Meredith Casey took the girls to the beach. Katherine and Charlotte later told me she drove fast and they didn't have to wear their seat belts. Michael and James III played Monopoly. My mother told Lillie to put Stephen in his stroller and take him for a long walk on the dirt road behind our house, and when she got to the beach, she was to help him collect stones and seashells. On the way back, when he would be asleep, she was to pick enough rose hips to fill the pouch of the stroller, and to only pick bright red ones. And it wasn't any of Lillie's business to know how she was going to spend the afternoon.

My mother would soak the rose hips in apple cider for a few days and then rub the mixture on her body, wrap herself in an old bath sheet, lie in the sun on a chaise longue for an hour, and then take an ice-cold outside shower. She said it took the poisons out and kept the skin soft. Beth took a nap, and I went grocery shopping.

My mother helped me with the breakfast dishes.

"Did you see how this Beth of yours came down to the table

this morning? Who wears makeup, especially in the summer? Does she realize how she looks? Old. All you need to do is keep your eyebrows shaped, put on lipstick, and keep your face clean and moist. She cuts her cuticles instead of pushing them back every time you wash your hands. These stupid American women don't know it's simplicity that makes you elegant. And I cannot tolerate a woman who keeps looking at herself in the mirror. When you pass a mirror, you never look at yourself. Ever. It looks so bad. If only you took care of yourself. You would show them. I told her son, in front of her, to take his feet off the couch. She thinks she's bringing up a gentleman?"

The Tuesday after Labor Day, Phillip flew back to Westchester with the Caseys, and I started readying the house for the winter. I removed the slipcovers from the couches and chairs, folded them, and put them in large cotton bags, sprinkling a handful of cloves in each to ward off mice. I did the same for the bedding. I rolled up the rag rugs and piled them up in the attic, one on top of the other, making two piles of seven after peeling the candy wrappers off the floor. I covered the hydrangeas with burlap to save them from the deer. I called in a chimney sweep, I pulled the geraniums out of the clay pots and brought the pots inside. I called Eli, the plumber, whose son Chris died in an auto accident the winter before and who himself would die the following year of a heart attack, to drain the pipes. I told Katherine and Charlotte that Scratchy went to live with a little boy who was lonely because he didn't have any pets.

We took the early morning ferry back. When it passed the lighthouse, we threw pennies into the water so we would be sure to come back, and we arrived home in the late afternoon.

The dense pines around the house on Sheppard Road wouldn't let in the sun, and the windows Phillip kept closed didn't let in the air, and there was a thin film of green mold over everything. I started to clean.

The Pianos

Katherine asked her father if she could start taking piano lessons, her friend played and she wanted to too. Two weeks later an ebony Steinway grand, Series B, arrived.

Phillip was walking down Fifty-Seventh Street and passed Steinway Hall. After his lunch meeting, he walked up Fifty-Seventh Street and went in. The salesperson played a Chopin nocturne on the piano he thought would have the gentle sound Phillip was looking for. It was beautiful, Phillip said. It made him want to learn to play.

The piano was delivered by the Harvey Brothers. It went into the middle room, as far away from the fireplace as possible.

Phillip, Michael, Katherine, and Charlotte started taking lessons from a teacher who lived in town.

Phillip practiced his scales every night before going to bed. He drank only on Saturdays and only after he played for hours.

"I don't understand it, Mrs. Calt," the piano teacher said to me when I arrived late one afternoon. I had spent fifteen minutes telling Charlotte to get out from under her bed and into the car. "Your husband manages to come here on time. Why can't you?"

"I'm sorry."

"Please don't let it happen again. My time's valuable."

I asked her if she had watched the Sunday broadcast of Vladimir Horowitz's return to Russia and his performance at the Moscow Conservatory.

"Yes, I did. He missed so many notes. If it were anyone else, they'd be laughed offstage."

I found another piano teacher for the children. Phillip auditioned for and was accepted by a concert pianist recommended by Mr. Seville. She said Phillip was gifted and should have started playing earlier.

Phillip took the Casio keyboard he had bought Michael one Christmas to practice on when we went to New Hampshire. I told him he shouldn't deny himself the pleasure of playing on a piano, especially when he worked so hard, and we bought another Steinway grand.

The Harvey Brothers tried getting it to the second floor, but it was too wide for the stairs. The window that took up the north wall and looked out to the ski mountain had to be taken out, and the piano hoisted and brought in. It was placed as far away from the fireplace as possible.

The children went to their ski lessons, and Phillip and I remained in the house. I'd hear him practice as I cleaned up. Sometimes I'd stop, sit down, and listen to the piece he would be working on. The piano had a beautiful sound, and his touch was light. We'd go to the mountain to meet the children for lunch.

The Renovation

We hired an architect, Giacomo Lorenzo, recommended by an associate of Phillip's. She said he had done a fabulous job on her downtown loft.

Giacomo's blueprints for Sheppard Road indicated knocking out four walls in the kitchen and a wall in the center room for more light, a stone terrace, a bath/laundry room in the basement, and a powder room near the front door. I wanted the bathrooms upstairs redone too, but Phillip said we had to wait. Giacomo interviewed general contractors and told us he felt Mr. Aurella had come in with a reasonable bid, and we hired him.

I convinced Phillip we should move into the Bedford house while Sheppard Road was being renovated. My mother stayed with the children on Nantucket and I went back to Westchester to pack. The Harvey Brothers moved us to Bedford a week before the start of school and the renovation.

I convinced Phillip to have the upstairs bathrooms redone. He wanted signed contracts specifying the work. I told him Mr. Aurella said he would work for time and material and it would save us a lot of money. They worked fast. Hadn't they torn down the kitchen in a day? Phillip brought in a major client, and even with twenty associates helping him, he barely kept up. He told me to go ahead and do the bathrooms the way I wanted.

The problems started with the bluestone for the terrace. They didn't match. The kitchen cabinets and appliances were installed two inches lower than industry standard because if they weren't, they'd be higher than the specially designed windows Giacomo had ordered from Germany. When it was remembered to install heat in the kitchen, one of the tall stone outside chimneys collapsed.

Joe, Mr. Aurella's tile man, and his assistant, Tony, turned out not to know how to lay tile.

We stood in an upstairs bathroom.

"I believe if you move these tiles a little over to the left and take the tiles that Mrs. Calt thinks are—" Giacomo was interrupted by Mr. Aurella's son.

"Mrs. Calt, your husband's on the phone."

"Amine? Why did it take you so long to get to the phone?"

"There's a problem in—"

"Tell them to get out."

"How's London?"

"What do you mean, how's London? My secretary has to call me here and tell me that bastard Aurella calls, calls my office looking for more money. Tell him to go fuck himself. Is that Giacomo there?"

"Everybody's fine."

"Play your fucking games, Amine. This is all your fault. I have to take the Concorde back Monday to make a meeting. Start opening your mouth. You can do it to me, do it to them." He hung up.

" 'Bye."

I went back upstairs. "I don't think this can be fixed."

"Sure it can be fixed. But if you want it the way you want it, it'll cost you five thousand more," said Joe. Giacomo and Mr. Aurella continued looking at the tiles.

"Why?" I asked. "It wasn't done right in the first place."

"Come on, Tony. Pack up. This lady doesn't know what she wants. Let's go."

A year went by, and the renovation was still not complete. I gained twenty pounds and couldn't stop smoking. I'd be late picking Michael up from high school to drive him back to the Bedford house. Sometimes he would be waiting outside for two hours. I told him it was difficult for me to make it on time, and I had no way of getting in touch with him when I was running late, and couldn't he just walk to the house on Sheppard Road? I used to walk to school, why couldn't he? "It's three miles." So? "The house is dark." Turn on the lights, and do your homework. Your father and I will take you back to Bedford after he goes over what's been done.

It was tough for Michael in the high school. Friendships were formed in the junior high, and he had been in a private school since first grade. And Sheppard Road was not in a neighborhood, the houses were separated by large pieces of property. He did join the high school ski team, but Phillip couldn't understand why Michael wasn't winning all the races. Hasn't he been skiing since he was ten? Haven't we been going up to New Hampshire every weekend so that he could become an expert skier? What was the matter with him? He skied fine in New Hampshire where it was tough, and here he was in a school where they could barely get down the hill, and he couldn't even finish first. What was his problem?

Michael wanted to go away to school and didn't care if he had to repeat tenth grade.

Charlotte's lovebirds died. First Cream, and a few days later Peaches. And then Bridges died in her sleep. I remembered when we lived in the small house and a baby-sitter for the couple who

lived on top of the hill came in to tell me Bridges had saved the little boy's life. If she hadn't seen it with her own eyes, she would
never have believed it. She had to go in for a minute, and she
left the little boy outside, and she saw him through the bathroom
window walking toward the road, and our dog was beside him,
knocking him to the ground. He'd get up, and she'd knock him
down again, pushing him away from the road.

Bridges was cremated. My mother said to bury her ashes—it
wasn't good to have them in the house. They're in a blue and white
porcelain jar I look at every day.

Phillip told me he wasn't spending any more money on the
renovation. "I want these clowns out of this house."

"It's almost done. Let them just finish."

"This has been going on for a year and a half. Every night I
meet you and ask why wasn't any progress made? And you keep
apologizing for these fucking bastards."

"Where were you?"

"I was working to make the money to pay for all this crap. I told
you I wanted a contract for the upstairs. And you said, 'No, trust them.
It'll be fine.' Do you know the banks are not extending us any more
credit? They now want the construction loan secured? They're de-
manding we remortgage Nantucket and Florida? This has cost us six
hundred thousand dollars so far. Where am I going to get the money?"

"Maybe we should sell this house and stay in Bedford."

"Why don't you go to hell."

It took less than a year after the Wall Street crash of 1987 for
the bottom to fall out of the real estate market. It was then that
Phillip told me I had ruined his life.

———

The Harvey Brothers moved our beds and a TV from Bedford back to Sheppard Road. Everything else was left in the Bedford house—we hoped it would make it more attractive to sell. The art teacher at the children's school needed a place to live, and I told her she could stay there until it sold.

Phillip took the children to New Hampshire, and I stayed home for the weekend to clean after the renovation. Going down to the laundry room Sunday morning, I saw the previous day's waste coming out of the floor drains. I had wanted the drains installed because hosing the dirt and pine needles that children track in into floor drains is a lot easier than cleaning the floors with a mop and buckets of water. Instead of connecting the drains to a dry well, Mr. Aurella's plumber had connected the floor drains to our septic system. During the renovation, paper towels had been used instead of toilet paper, causing a clog in the system.

A month later the associate with the downtown loft was called in Australia where she, Phillip, and three others were on a business trip and was told that her shower had collapsed into the apartment below and she should come home. Giacomo hadn't indicated any type of waterproofing in his blueprints.

Phillip told me Giacomo had called him at the office and asked if we would allow a magazine to take pictures of the house. If we did, Giacomo wouldn't demand the rest of the money we owed him. I told Phillip to tell him no.

A retired engineer presiding over our arbitration heard from Mr. Aurella's son's friend's husband that we were planning to move out of our house, and therefore what reason did he have for awarding damages? Phillip said we'd have to spend an additional seventy thousand dollars to fix the whole mess.

We finally sold the Bedford house at a loss to Robert Keenan, his wife, and their triplets. He was the oldest son of Mrs. Keenan and had grown up in the house. They were happy nothing had to be done to it.

To help pay for the renovation, we thought we should sell

Florida too. We lowered the price several times and received an offer that was withdrawn when the offerer was arrested for drug smuggling. We then rented the house to a family who kept their three Dobermans secret from us and locked in the garage. The neighbors complained, and they left. Their security deposit was used for repairs. A young couple bought it while the work was being done on it. He was opening a brokerage firm in the office complex that had replaced a grapefruit grove. They planned to put a second story on the house and get a catamaran they could haul onto the beach.

I took Ret for his morning walk. He chased a deer and killed it. A few months earlier he had wandered over to a condominium development nearby, and a little girl had brought him in to play with her new puppy. Ret took the puppy's neck in his mouth and shook the puppy until its neck broke.

When I came back from the walk, Phillip hadn't left for work. I told him what had happened, and he told me it was my fault for not having Ret on a leash. I told him I thought if I went walking with Ret when no one was around, nothing would happen.

"I guess you were wrong."

In the afternoon I took Ret to the vet and had him put down.

Vermont

I called Carole and told her I'd take her up on the offer of staying with her at her cousin's place in Vermont. Katherine and Charlotte could look after Stephen while I was gone for a few days, and Phillip would be there at night.

The farmhouse stood on top of a hill outside Manchester. Carole decided we should ski Stratton instead of Bromley—it had more trails and had a great shop for hot chocolate.

"It's amazing you got out of the house. Jesus, it wouldn't hurt them if they went out to eat. You know, Amine, no one's going to remember anyway."

Carole came over once, early in the morning, to wish me a happy birthday. She brought my present with her—a pail full of cleaning supplies. She told me to stand at attention, and from her sweater pocket she pulled out a large medal she got at a tag sale and pinned it to my breast. She said it was in recognition for my long and devoted service: "And when it becomes too much for you, you can stop and wipe your brow." From her other pocket she pulled out a white linen handkerchief with the initial A embroidered in a corner. My mother told me never to accept a handkerchief as a present—it meant the end of a friendship and tears. I told Carole it was lovely and I'd cherish it.

"Carole, Phillip wants Katherine to go to a ski academy."

"You're kidding."

"He says it would be the best for her."

"Simple. You just don't let her do it. Private school ruins kids. Let her have a normal life. You sent them all to that school in Greenwich where they learned absolutely nothing. Thank god it only goes up to the eighth grade. And you have Michael in that useless prep school and now you want to send her away too. She stays home, that's it. End of story."

We made a bed near the wood-burning stove. It snowed during the night, in the morning I threw in another log and the room quickly got warm.

"I'm taking you out for breakfast. I want to have pancakes. Lizzy told me there's a country store where they make the best pancakes with yeast and buttermilk and real maple syrup."

We went skiing after we had the pancakes. It was a Tuesday, and there was hardly anyone on the trails. We took five runs, laughing the whole time. It started to snow, and we stopped at the country store and had pancakes again. The wood-burning stove was still on when we came in. We fell asleep. In the morning, on our way back to Westchester, we stopped at the country store and ate those dense, sour, sweet pancakes.

Katherine wanted to go to the local high school and take gymnastics.

"Amine, all the coaches say Katherine can make it all the way. She's phenomenal. It's not enough anymore that she skis weekends. If she wants to be the best, she's got to ski every day. She can make it. We're going to give her this chance. I never got it as a kid, and you certainly didn't. I want her to have it. Do you know the colleges that will want her?"

"What about Charlotte?"

"Charlotte can go too, next year."

"I don't mean that. I mean they're very close. What's going to happen to Charlotte without Katie?"

We bought Katherine a golden retriever puppy—she named her Molly. The school wouldn't let her bring Molly. They said if they let her, they'd have to let everyone else. I told her I'd take good care of Molly and we'd bring her with us every time we came up. We drove Katherine to school and got her settled in the room she would be sharing with three other girls. I got her a sheepskin mattress cover, a down comforter, four down pillows, and white flannel sheets for her bed, to keep her warm.

Phillip went to work every day, dreading calls from creditors.

Piano Camp

I went to work for Mr. Henry a few days at the end of each month, closing the books for his mail-order business. Mr. Henry sent out humorous prints of men playing golf to anyone who called or replied by mail to the ads he placed in travel magazines. His office used to be his daughter's bedroom and was in the back of the house. The peeling bark of a huge oak could be seen through the window that stood between two desks. The left arm of the couch stopped the door to the room from closing. A yellowed pillow lay at one end of the couch, and a throw, in Mrs. Henry's family tartan, lay at the other. A bookcase with atlases and boxes of letterhead from Mr. Henry's old Madison Avenue firm stood by the door to the turquoise-and-pink-tiled bathroom.

Mr. Henry was tall and gaunt and wore a bow tie and a long-sleeved shirt regardless of the season. He'd stand when I'd come into the room, and he'd say, "Mrs. Calt, a pleasure," bowing slightly.

Their square, wood-shingled house stood on a hill overlooking Quaker Road. Mrs. Henry told me their house and the cottage across the way with the yew hedges around it had been the only ones here fifty years ago. After their son and daughter left home, Mrs. Henry had started baby-sitting. During the day the mothers would bring their children to her, and at night she'd go to them. She had been a nurse at Flower Fifth Avenue before she married Mr. Henry.

In the mornings Mrs. Henry would sit in her armchair by the large, unwashed window in the living room, drinking black coffee and reading the *Times*; the cats slept on the radiator beside her. A portrait of her father hung in a wide gold frame above the stone fireplace. Cats had scratched the velvet backs of the two couches. It had taken Mrs. Henry three years to needlepoint the covers of the two Queen Anne chairs. She used gold thread for the bees and sixteen shades of purple for the violets.

I'd quickly pass the cat litter box in the front hall by the kitchen door and walk toward the fragrance of Joy that Mrs. Henry used every morning after her bath. She wore slacks and kept a handkerchief tucked under the cuff of her silk blouse. Her feet, in cloth slippers, rested on a footstool. She was ninety-four and a few years older than her husband.

"It's always so nice to see you, Amine."

"It's always so nice to see you, Mrs. Henry."

"Alan is in his study. Let him wait a little while longer. Sit here with me. Tell me, how is your family?"

"Everybody's good."

"Your husband?"

"Phillip's in Vermont, at a piano camp."

"Piano camp? I never knew such a thing existed."

"Yes, it's in Vermont. A family runs it. They're all concert pianists. They have this huge house, and every room has a piano in it. Katie and Charlotte went there one summer."

"Did they like it?"

"They did. They were there for two weeks. When I came to pick them up, they looked gray. They told me they had Pop-Tarts for breakfast and hot dogs for lunch and dinner. And they could walk downtown anytime they wanted to to buy candy."

"Did they learn to play well?"

"They did. They loved their teacher. She's beautiful—she's the oldest daughter."

"Does Phillip have her?"

"No, she moved to Minnesota with her husband. There are four people taking this special course with Phillip. He plays beautifully. But you know, Mrs. Henry, whatever Phillip does, he does well. He's a genius. And he's very disciplined."

"You must be proud of him."

"I am."

"Amine, it's a shame you have let yourself go. You should lose weight, my dear. Besides, it's very bad for your health."

"I know I should. I'm fine during the day. It's the nights. I can't stop eating at night."

"Has Katie left for the ski academy?"

"She has."

"How is Charlotte?"

"It's hard for her. They're very close."

"She'll be fine."

"I think so, Mrs. Henry. You know, Mrs. Henry, she always followed Katie, whatever Katie did. There are home movies of them—Katie's running and Charlotte's running behind her, and Katie will quickly change direction, and Charlotte will change direction too, with her. And now I see she's more—she's good. Yes, I think she's going to be fine. And how are you, Mrs. Henry?"

"I was sitting here and regretting."

"You were? About what?"

"Alan never liked sex very much, and I was remembering all the men I had met and how I should have gone to bed with every one of them."

During the week Phillip comes home at eight and goes upstairs to change. He'll hang his suit on a hanger, or if he's worn it three times, he'll drop it in the basket for dry cleaning. He'll put on a pair of jeans and a T-shirt.

He'll come down to the kitchen and go to the freezer for the bottle of vodka. He'll fill a tall glass with ice and pour the thick, colorless liquid to the top. He's gotten into the habit of not eating breakfast or lunch, and the effect of vodka on an empty stomach is immediate. I'll ask him how his day went, and he'll answer me with a word.

His chair is beside the wood-burning stove. His glass is on the bird's-eye maple table beside him. The television is on CNN, and he'll go back to reading the paper he began on the train home.

He prefers to have his dinner in his chair, and I serve him food that doesn't require a knife for cutting. I'll place his plated dinner on a large white linen napkin covering his lap. Sometimes he'll motion for me to set his plate on the island, and it is on those nights that he'll fall asleep in his chair. He doesn't practice on the piano during the week anymore—he says he's too tired. He plays for a few hours on the weekends.

Charlotte slams the door. It means Jerome had them go all out at practice. He's getting them ready for the Princeton meet, and he wants her fly to get faster. I've sat in the stands and seen her have dry heaves after a grueling set. "You're a beautiful girl, inside and out," I'll whisper to her as she sleeps.

She throws her swim bag containing seven chlorine-faded swimsuits, two empty water bottles, a pair of paddles, a pair of fins, four pairs of goggles, empty wrappers from the Twizzlers she tries not to buy, and a pair of hot pink plastic clogs down the stairs to the laundry room and pours herself a glass of organic orange juice from the crystal pitcher standing on the island.

"How was practice?" Phillip asks as I reach into the oven for her warm dinner plate.

"It was hard. Mom, I'm not hungry. I'm not eating anything."

"Eat this now, Missy, because later the kitchen will be closed. Charlotte, sit down."

"Pop."

No answer.

"Pop. I want to quit swimming. Jerome is such an asshole. I can't stand him. I'm sick of the whole thing. I want to quit."

"Quit."

"I'm going to."

"Why don't you? And be like your mother, who hasn't accomplished anything in her life."

An apple tart I made that morning was in front of me as I stood at the island. I cut a large piece and ate it, not bothering to get a plate or a fork.

Best Doctor

Phillip told me we were two months behind in paying the mortgage on Sheppard Road and we needed twenty-five thousand dollars. He told me to ask my mother to lend it to us. If she had to cash in a CD, we would pay the penalty for cashing it in early, and we would pay her ten percent interest on it, and we'd pay her back in a year.

It took a week for me to get up the nerve to call her. I didn't give her a reason for wanting it.

Without hesitating she said no. She told me she worked hard for her money. It wasn't her fault we lived like millionaires—what would happen to her money if we went bankrupt?

"I've never asked you for anything."

Her voice became soft and quiet. "I'm sorry. I can't."

Phillip sold his sixty-thousand-dollar boat to George for twenty-five and threw in two fishing rods and their reels for catching tuna. We rented the townhouse in New Hampshire to a couple with no children who lived in Boston. The rent covered the mortgage.

I didn't talk to my mother for months.

"Natalie, what do you think? Should I call Mom and ask her to come to Nantucket?"

"Mom has cancer." And after a long pause, "She didn't want you to know. I'm flying down to see some doctors with her."

I dialed a wrong number three times.

"Mama."

"Aminachka."

"I'm going to be with you."

"No. You'll come if I need an operation."

I flew to Los Angeles a week later, a day before my mother was admitted to Cedars-Sinai. I took a cab to the cottage on Mrs. Chase's Bell-Air estate. My mother prepared the beet salad I loved. It was the first time I saw her without lipstick. We sat outside on the lawn near a brick wall of flowering jasmine.

"Amine, why did this happen to me? I did everything right."

I put down the white throw I was knitting when the surgeon came out and sat across from me. He told me he was sorry it had taken so long, but they had to wait for the pathology report. Two lymph nodes were involved. I hadn't realized I'd gotten my period, and I'd bled through to the beige upholstered seat. I wrapped the throw around me and carried the chair to my mother's hospital room to try to get the stain out. A cot was brought in for me to sleep on, and I watched as nurses came and went. During the day I'd take a break and go to the cottage to feed her parrot, Vanya. He had flown in through her open window one afternoon as she was ironing.

After my mother's release, I stayed with her in the cottage. She insisted on getting out of bed to feed Vanya and to change her colostomy bag. She said she didn't need a nurse.

"I am not going to have chemotherapy. It's poison. Maybe I'll have the radiation."

"Mom. You can't make up your own rules on this. When you follow the treatment, the cure rate is ninety percent."

"Did you hear me? Chemotherapy is poison. They put poison in you. I shouldn't have had the operation. There was one doctor who said I should just have radiation. I should have listened to him. Once they open you up, air gets in and it spreads. This one just wanted to experiment on me."

"Mom, you had the best doctor in California. He used lasers to operate on you so that your recovery would be quicker."

"Amine, why are you so naïve? Do you know the medical profession? I do. So don't talk to me about it. You'll stay with me for another few days. Then you'll go back. It's not necessary for you to be here. I can take care of myself. Ella said she'd come, she's in Westwood, and Jean is here. I'm fine." She looked tired.

"Come to New York with me."

"Why are you so stubborn? I'm staying here until I get my strength, and then I'll come for the summer."

On Nantucket I convinced my mother to have the chemotherapy. We went to an oncologist in Westchester.

"I'm deciding what to do, not you. I've spent the summer with you. That's enough for me. I am not staying in Westchester. You have too much to do without driving me back and forth and waiting for me. When I think about it, it gets me upset. Jean told me I can stay in the cottage for as long as I want. She wants me to take care of the main house. She knows everything will be done the way it's supposed to be done."

"Mom. Dr. Mann is the best oncologist in New York. He's right here at Northern Westchester, and he's at Sloan-Kettering. It's nothing for me to take you."

"Don't tell me it's nothing. You don't have time. I see what you do, and it gets me upset. When I don't see it, I don't know. You don't have anyone helping you now, not that you ever let anyone help you. No. I'm going back to Los Angeles, so I don't see it."

"Mom. Please."

"I said no."

Jean asked Andy, who used to be Mrs. Chase's chauffeur, to come back and live in the apartment above the garage and drive my mother to the UCLA Medical Center for her treatments. Jean said her mother would have wanted it that way. My mother told me she cooked dinner for Andy to thank him for taking her, and he played the saxophone at a jazz club on weekends. The chemotherapy and radiation lasted for months. I called my mother every day.

"Mom, how do you feel?"

"Good."

"It's good that you're going through with it."

"It's a big mistake."

"Mom, it's the best thing—the doctors said—"

"Don't tell me what the doctors said. Do you think they know anything? Especially the American ones?"

"Come here after you finish."

"I'm not going to Nantucket this summer."

"Why not?"

"I'm going to Russia. You won't come with me, will you?"

"Mom, I have to—"

"Don't say it. You have to take care of children who can take care of themselves. It's not normal to love them the way you do. I'll go alone. Maybe I'll come to Nantucket the last two weeks in August and come back with you to New York. I want to see a Russian doctor in New York I read about."

Something Else

Dr. Vladimir Tarhanov's office was on the ground floor of a pre-war building on West Seventy-Ninth Street. He met us in the lobby and walked us into a dimly lit room. He sat behind a mahogany partner's desk, clear of everything except for a notepad and pen. Thick dark brown drapes were drawn across the window behind him. The room smelled of bergamot.

In a quiet voice he told my mother, in Russian, she would start getting up at five in the morning. After massaging her body with sesame oil, she would do forty-five minutes of yoga following the instructor on the tape he would later give her. She would then dress in comfortable clothing, made of cotton, and go for an hour-long walk, walking only on ground that's unpaved. She would keep distilled water, boiled for twenty minutes in an enameled pot, in a two-gallon Thermos she could purchase at Hammacher Schlemmer, and she would drink the water, in an eight-ounce crystal glass, throughout the day. She was not to have anything to eat or drink after six P.M. She was to eat small pieces of fruit, excluding coconut and pineapple, before each meal, and she was to eat only items on the list. Fruits and vegetables had to soak twenty minutes in boiled, cooled, distilled water and were to be rinsed in bottled spring water before they were minimally cooked. She was never to eat meat again, and she was to give herself a coffee enema, through her colostomy, every night before going to sleep. If she did what he told her to do, she would undo the harm done by the chemotherapy and radiation. She would be healthy again.

My mother sat on an antique cane chair by his desk. I sat close by on a leather couch facing a large Chagall oil of a woman on a horse, flying through the air, a ring of flowers on her head, and I believed he was our salvation.

In the car on the way back to Westchester, my mother told me to stop at a corner store.

"Mom, they don't sell organic vegetables there."

"I want chocolate."

"Didn't you hear what the doctor said to you?"

"What that man said was nonsense. I thought he had something else to say."

"You have to follow exactly what he said."

"Amine, stop at that store."

I didn't.

My mother left for California at the end of September, and I went to see the doctor.

He sat on one couch and I sat on the other.

"Your name suits you. You know its meaning?"

"Yes. It means trust."

"Do you know your maiden name also means trust?"

"I didn't."

"My mother was Tatar."

"She was? Was she from Kazan?"

"Your father was from Kazan."

"Yes."

"It is amazing. And here we are. Tell me why have you come to see me?" His hand kept gliding over a bronze figurine.

"I want to lose weight. But Doctor, I don't know if I'll be able to follow your regime. I'm not a very disciplined person."

"Amine, you are a very disciplined person. You're just a free spirit." I looked at him and wondered if that could be true. "I would like to see you at least twice a month."

I bought the Thermos. I started drinking the boiled, distilled water, adding the juice of half a lemon to each glass. I woke up at five and immediately got out of bed. I gave myself a massage with sesame oil. I did the yoga, walked, took cold showers, bought a linen dress, and ate only what was on the list, and I began to lose weight.

I met Sarah at the Museum of Modern Art—she was representing a Russian filmmaker at the New Directors' Film Festival. The three of us continued our discussion at a nearby restaurant. He went back to St. Petersburg, and Sarah and I became friends. Having lunch one afternoon, she told me of an idea she had for a screenplay: a woman, a younger man, she's Russian, he's American, the husband lives in Moscow. Sarah asked if I would like to help her write it. I told her I had never written anything, I couldn't spell. It was hard for me to even write notes for the children's school absences. I did keep a diary when I was eight, but . . . I didn't start reading until I was ten and had recurring nightmares of not finishing high school. She said none of that mattered, and we'd have fun. I told her I didn't think I could do it every day. She said she couldn't either. We could work in her apartment, twice a week. Her building was across from Lincoln Center, right off the West Side Highway.

Carole called. "Amine, where have you been? You're never home."

"I'm here."

"No, you're not."

"I've been going into the city."

"To do what?"

"I'm helping a friend write a screenplay."

"Talk about wasting time. Anyway, Eloise wants the name of your doctor. She needs to lose weight."

"Carole, you know, you should go see him. He could help you."

"I don't need a doctor, my pressure's fine. Anyway, I would never do what you do. It's too weird. Is he at least good looking?"

"Yes."

Dr. Tarhanov's parents were sent to Siberia where they died of tuberculosis. He was allowed to return to Moscow when he was fourteen, and he lived with four others in the basement of an abandoned synagogue. He became a doctor and emigrated in 1978. He met someone here, but they separated a year ago. His one regret was that he never had children.

I lost sixty pounds. Phillip said I was beginning to look good again. Dr. Tarhanov said I looked like his mother when she was a young girl.

"I'm going to give you an oil. At night, when you are ready for bed, you will place three drops of it on your fingertips and gently massage it in. The place where you massage it in is very important. Let me show you. Please stand. It should be right here." He touched me just above my pubic bone. "You will do this every night until the bottle is empty."

"The oil is for?"

"It will heighten your desires."

"My desires?"

"Your desires as a woman."

I sat down. "Dr. Tarhanov, my husband and I are rarely together. He works very late, and he's tired when he comes home."

"I'm sorry. Then, of course, you shouldn't use it."

I had a cold. Dr. Tarhanov asked for the exact time of my birth, and gave me a remedy. The cold went away.

I had trouble sleeping. He told me to boil fresh ginger in milk for twenty minutes and drink it before going to bed. I started sleeping through the night.

A neighbor's dog bit Stephen on the hand. After the wound was sutured by a plastic surgeon in the emergency room, Dr. Tarhanov told me the ingredients for a salve and said Stephen's scar would disappear in a year.

Eloise started seeing him and told a few of her friends about him. They all lost weight. I asked Eloise if she'd come with me to my next scheduled appointment. I was relieved when she said yes.

We ate lunch before going in to see him.

"Isn't it amazing, Amine, if you looked at him, you'd never think he could do anything for you. Doesn't he look like a giant midget? And have you noticed his shoes? Mom always says to stay away from short men and to always look at the shoes people wear. Amine... I'm sorry. I shouldn't have said that. He has changed my life. I mean, I feel great. I've already lost fifteen pounds, and my hair is thicker. What does it matter what he looks like? Right?"

"Dr. Tarhanov told me a very funny story the last time I went to see him. He was a medical student at the university in Moscow, and there was a flu epidemic, and all the medical students had to go to check on the sick people in their apartments. He went to an apartment where a beautiful woman lived with her parents. She was in bed, and he asked her if he could listen to her heart. He took out his stethoscope and told her to pull down the straps of her nightgown. He told me he tried very hard to maintain his composure. He put the flat part of the stethoscope on her breast and listened and she said to him, 'Doctor, wouldn't it be better if you put the ends in your ears?'" Eloise and I laughed.

"Do you speak Russian together?"

"Yes."

"That is so cool. Mom should go see him."

"She won't. She doesn't believe in it. Look at what he's done for us. I think he's great. Don't you feel great?"

"Yes. Mom told me not to mention it to Dad—he'd really flip out if he knew. I bet Dr. Tarhanov could have saved Grandma Didi."

"I'm sure of it."

"Amine, did I ever tell you my favorite Grandma Didi story? It was when I was thirteen, and we were in the car, Mom, Grandma Didi, and I. Grandma Didi was in the front with Mom, and I was in the back. Mom forgets something and goes back into the house, and Grandma Didi turns around and asks me if I have a boyfriend. And I say no, like I'm going to have a boyfriend at thirteen. And she says, good. Because all they want to do is fuck ya, fuck ya, fuck ya."

Eloise and I laughed.

Thanksgiving

My affair with the doctor started a week before my mother came to live with us.

Sarah and I had finished writing for the day. Charlotte didn't need to be picked up from swim practice, and Stephen was going to a friend's house for dinner. I called him from a pay phone on the street to say I was close to running out of the tea he had given me. He told me to come over.

He sat at his desk, and I sat on the couch. He talked about an exciting case he had, a young woman with a mysterious rash over her entire body, especially on her face. He had formulated a salve from ingredients sent to him from Japan, and she was getting better.

I called him when I got to Westchester.

"I feel strange. I don't know what it is."

"Will you come here tomorrow at nine?"

"In the morning?"

"Yes."

He was standing under the blue awning of his building. He crossed the street to the garage, opened the car door for me, and told the attendant to charge it to his account. He took my hand, and we walked to his office.

He apologized for coming too quickly, he hadn't been with a woman in over two years; next time would be longer, and it would get better and better. He went into the small kitchen and pulled out, from the refrigerator, a dozen pale pink roses.

"I wanted them to match the color of the blouse you wore the day you showed me where you take your morning walks. You and I were on the path by the river, and I fell in love with you."

Afterward I drove him to Bloomingdale's so he could return an iron that had stopped working.

When I got to Westchester, I left a message on his answering machine, how wonderful he made me feel and what a marvelous man he was. Wasn't it wonderful that we could say such beautiful things to each other in Russian?

The next morning, after driving Charlotte and Stephen to school, I left for the city. Sarah and I worked till two, and when she went out to take some film to be developed, I called him and asked if he could see me. I left the car in the garage underneath Sarah's building and took a cab to his office. He met me at his door, and over his shoulder I saw one of the couches pulled out into a bed.

He knew I had faked it.

"Darling, it'll come."

"How did you know?"

"I am one with you."

"Will I ever be able to?"

"Of course you will. It is all about trust. Trusting the man you're with. In time, darling, you will trust me. And Amine, you will."

I took a cab back to the garage and shopped for dinner on the way back. Stephen was in front of the TV waiting for me to take him to swim practice.

I called Vladimir the next morning from the garage and asked if I could see him. He said he couldn't, but maybe tomorrow. I drove back to Westchester. I called him the next morning from a pay phone off the Saw Mill River Parkway.

"Darling, it may not be possible today. I am very busy. Unfortunately, love, you chose a man who is involved with very sick people, who take up his time. Why don't you call me tomorrow, and we'll see each other then?"

"I can't. It's the weekend."

Phillip came through the bathroom on his way to the dressing room while I was taking a bath. I could see him standing in front of his bureau, gathering the loose change from his pockets and dropping the coins in the top right-hand drawer.

"Amine."

"Um."

"You were in the city again today?"

"I was working with Sarah."

"How long is this going to go on?" He waited until I finished rinsing my hair. "Don't you think every day is excessive? You'd better get your priorities straight. Your family comes first. If it doesn't, we're headed for a divorce."

Michael and Katherine drove down from school for the holidays. Natalie and her boyfriend flew in. When everyone was asleep I called Vladimir and got his answering machine.

The next morning I went to the airport to pick up my mother. I watched her walk up the ramp from the plane, a long dark brown cashmere coat draped over her shoulders and a light green chiffon scarf hanging from her neck. Her hair was colored a tone darker, or did it just seem that way? Her small purse with the long strap crisscrossed her chest, and in her gloved hand she carried the blue case with her parrot, Vanya, inside. When I kissed her, she smelled metallic. "Mom, I have to make a quick phone call, and I'll be right back. If you see your bags, don't pick them up. They'll come around again, and I'll do it."

"Amine, hurry back. I can't stand too long."

She sat next to me in the car with the blue case on her lap. Vanya was silent.

"Mom, I fixed up the attic. It's really lovely. We got you a double bed. I made a little sitting area with the two couches. Carole gave me a beautiful needlepoint rug for the bathroom. Phillip brought up the TV from our room and a VCR. Michael hooked up his stereo for you. Everybody's home, waiting for you. Katherine and Michael. Natalie and Barry. I got a big cage for Vanya."

"You've lost a lot of weight."

"I'm on the doctor's regime."

"What doctor?"

"The Russian doctor we went to see."

"Did I tell you I made five hundred dollars on my tag sale?"

"That's good, Mom."

"I'm going to buy the children something. How much weight did you lose?"

"I lost sixty pounds."

"Don't lose any more—your face will get too thin, and that's not good. Finally, you're doing something with yourself. How's Katya?"

"She's good. You'll see."

"It's idiocy, her skiing. Do you know what it's doing to her health? You remember my words. You need to exercise, but what she is doing is crazy. She's ruining her health. It's not good."

"Mom, she wants to do it."

"She wants to do it."

"Maybe it's good for her to be away. You tell me I do too much for them. Maybe it'll make her independent, and isn't that good?"

"Don't be a fool."

On Thanksgiving Day I got up at five and took a walk with Molly. When I got back, my mother was in the kitchen, and the batter for the pancakes was made, and the dining-room table was set for breakfast. After we ate, she told everyone dinner would be at four.

Phillip went to the office for a few hours. The children went with Natalie and Barry to the movies, and my mother and I stayed in the kitchen. She wanted a dozen yellow pears for the center of the table, and when I went to find them, I called Vladimir and left a message. We sat down to dinner at four. Barry was in love with Natalie, but she wasn't in love with him. Phillip had already had a couple of vodkas. Kate didn't want to talk about skiing. Stephen ate fast so he and Michael could go out and play catch, and Charlotte braided Katie's hair. My mother looked tired, and I wondered what excuse I could use to go out to call him. I kept getting his machine. On Sunday I drove Natalie and Barry to the airport. Michael drove Katherine to the ski academy and then continued on to Bowdoin where he was majoring in economics. Charlotte went with friends to the mall, and Stephen played in his room. Phillip watched TV in the kitchen.

"Phillip," my mother said, "for tomorrow night, do you want me to make you beef Stroganoff? Do you like noodles? Or should I make it for you with kasha?" When he went up to bed, she said to me, "Amine, at least now he's drinking vodka instead of that poison scotch of his. With vodka you know what you're getting. I don't trust what they do with that scotch. I'm going to feed him as soon as he gets home. If he eats, it won't affect him."

I called Vladimir from the kitchen late that night.

"I finally got you."

"I'm sorry, I just got back."

"You were away?"

"I gave a lecture in San Francisco. I got back this afternoon."

"I'm sorry to be calling so late."

"It's all right, darling. I love hearing your voice. I played your messages over and over."

"Are you still working?"

"My last patient just left. How are you?"

"I'm fine. My mother's here with me. She's a little tired, but I think otherwise she's all right. She looks good. I'll be in the city tomorrow. Is there any chance I might see you?"

"It's possible. Why don't you call me when you get in."

"I promised Phillip I'd make him beef Stroganoff tonight. I need a pound and a half of fillet. And I need mushrooms—get the nice brown ones from Italy. Everything's better in Europe. It's chemicals and money here. I miss Daitch Shopwell. Their butter was the best. They had it in big chunks." She was standing by the island and wiping her hands on the dish towel she kept over her left shoulder. "Amine, I need sour cream. Get a small container of Breakstone's. Don't ever buy the big containers. When will you be home?"

"By seven?"

"That's too late. I can make the Stroganoff for Phillip, but what about the children? It's all right. I'll find something. I'll tell Charlotte to walk to town if I need anything, and she can go to that market that's owned by those crooks. I'll never forget when Katya was born, you lived in that small house. Remember? I walked to town. A lovely lady gave me a ride. I needed carrots for the chicken soup. He said eighty-nine cents for a bunch of carrots. I said to him, 'Eighty-nine cents?' He said yes. He looked right at me. Right into my eyes. He didn't think I would go over to where the carrots were. Sixty-nine cents. The sign was right there. Oh, what a crook. I said to him, 'The sign says sixty-nine cents,' and he said, 'Oh. The prices change all the time. I don't have time to change the signs.' Can you imagine? I'll go myself. They won't cheat me."

"Okay, Mom."

"Aminachka, you look so wonderful. I'm glad you're going into the city. Finally, you are doing something for yourself."

"Mom, I really like it."

"I want to give you money. I want you to buy something beautiful for yourself."

"Mom, it's okay."

"No, it's not okay. I want to do it and you're going to let me."

I used the pay phone in the garage to call him. He told me he'd be finished by one. Sarah was sitting at the computer, going over the dialogue we had written before Thanksgiving, when I walked into her room. I told her I had to leave by twelve-thirty, my mother was overwhelmed.

I took the car out of the garage of Sarah's building and parked in the garage across the street from his office. It would give me fifteen more minutes to be with him.

I gave Vladimir a picture Phillip had taken of me when we lived in Brooklyn Heights. The brownstone was in shadow, and I stood in the sunlight on a cold Sunday afternoon. I wore the shearling Phillip had bought for me when we were in Amsterdam. I only wore it that winter. The building where I had left the coat in storage burned down.

Vladimir gave me a short, tight black Donna Karan slip made of Lycra. I wore my mother's black suede heels. I wrapped her pearls around him, caressing him for a long, long time.

"Do you know pearls die? Someone once gave me a strand of pearls belonging to Czaritza Alexandra Fyodorovna. They wanted them brought back to life."

"Did you bring them back?"

"They were magnificent."

I got home at seven-thirty. There were warm slices of turkey, mashed potatoes, and a salad in covered dishes on the stove. Stephen had missed swim practice, Charlotte was in her room, and Phillip hadn't come home yet.

I went up to the attic. My mother was lying on the bed in her clothes. She told me she had called Sarah's to tell me to buy the fillet on the way home. She was too tired to walk to town, and Charlotte hadn't come home after school. Where was I? I told her I had left Sarah's early and there had been a lot of traffic on the Saw Mill River Parkway. There was an accident.

Things That Last

Sarah and I began working every day. I couldn't wait for the early afternoon to be over—there might be a chance I'd see him. Every time Sarah left the room to do something or to get something, I would try to reach him.

In the middle of December my mother called at Sarah's and told me to come home. She wasn't feeling well.

One day my mother was in the kitchen preparing a meal, and the next day she couldn't walk down the stairs.

I called Vladimir every day. He asked if she would listen to meditation tapes. She listened to Rachmaninoff and read Bunin instead. She would spray Chanel No. 5 whenever she had to change the plastic bag where her bowel emptied out.

After the New Year she told me she had to go to the hospital. I tied a large cashmere scarf around her head, and she held on to me as we made our way slowly down the stairs. We went back to

Northern Westchester. Dr. Mann told us the cancer had spread to her liver. While my mother was in the waiting room, getting on her coat, I went back into his office. I asked him what it meant. He said my mother had maybe six more months.

We drove to Sheppard Road in silence. I got her into bed and put two pillows under her knees and massaged her hands with rich cream.

"Aminachka, dearest, I think you should get a hospital bed for me."

I couldn't stop crying as I lay in bed next to Phillip. He told me to get hold of myself.

When Phillip fell asleep, I went into the kitchen and called Vladimir.

"My darling, nothing is terminal. Let me make a few phone calls, and we'll talk tomorrow morning."

In the morning after I spoke with Vladimir, I went up to the attic with my mother's breakfast.

"Mom, the doctor said you and I should go to Germany to see a friend of his."

"What are you talking about?"

"The Russian doctor. He told me that about five years ago he was very sick and this man cured him. This man is a specialist. He has his own hospital, and he knows what he's doing. He's a specialist, Mom, a German doctor. He has people all over the world coming to him. He does research."

"Where in Germany?"

Two days later, at the airport, waiting for our flight to Hamburg, I called Vladimir.

"You are sure he'll see my mother?"

"Of course. I talked to Oscar again last night. He is expecting you. The hotel is across the street from his office. I spoke with Frau

Hesse, and she has set aside the front room for you, the room I had. It has its own bath. You will be very comfortable. Call me collect as soon as you arrive. Do not worry. There is no finer doctor. Please promise me that you will not worry. Everything will be all right. Your mother will play with our child. I love you. Now hang up, or you'll miss your flight. Be safe. I love you."

The German doctor, after examining my mother in his office, admitted her to his hospital. The large window and the door to the balcony of her room were kept open during the day, and you saw the lake with a red swan house floating near shore.

"Amine, this is the way a hospital should be. The windows can open, you can wash the floor. Do you see how stupid it is to put carpeting in a hospital? Look at that woman. One woman with just a mop and a pail cleans the entire floor. It smells clean, the way it should. You take your own medicine, no one hands it to you, you leave when you want, no one is afraid of being sued. I don't want you to stay here with me. You don't know what you're breathing. Go outside and breathe some fresh air, and bring me something to eat. I can't stand these sausages. Buy something for yourself. The Germans make things that last."

I stayed in a small hotel near the hospital. Breakfast was served in the bar downstairs that smelled of stale beer and cigarettes. Phillip called and told me the schools had closed for a few days because of the freezing weather, but he managed to get to work. Everything was fine, the children missed me.

I saw a little boy sitting on a park bench, in the rain, speaking Russian to his drunk father. There was no sun, everything was gray, no one picked up the dog shit from the sidewalks. I found a Turkish restaurant that had the eggplant caviar my mother liked. Everyone on the streets looked whipped, and everything except my mother's room smelled of cigarettes and boiled cabbage. Her room smelled of Chanel No. 5 and of the flowers I brought her every day.

My mother pretended she didn't understand the doctors and

nurses speaking German. She was fourteen when they came into Minsk. She had three younger brothers. Her father had been a general in the Soviet army, and he had his family evacuated to the forest east of the city. In 1936 he fought in Spain with the Republicans and bought gold watches. In 1942, when there weren't any more gold watches left to sell, my grandmother became the cook for the German commandant. He allowed her to keep her sons, but my mother had to be sent to Germany, along with tens of thousands of other young girls, to a forced labor camp. The commandant told my grandmother her daughter wouldn't survive the camp, and he arranged for my mother to be sent to Berlin, to his parents who were doctors, and my mother became their kitchen maid. Toward the end of the war, on a day when she was told to go to the store, the commandant's parents committed suicide. Berlin was being bombed by the Americans and English, and my mother became one of many digging out the living and the dead in return for food.

"Amine, I remember I had just reached the air raid shelter. I ran to it. I skipped from one piece of broken concrete to another as if . . . The bombs were dropping, and I wasn't afraid. That's what youth does. I remember I was on the second step down, and a bomb exploded, and the woman behind me—her head rolled past me down the stairs. I came into the shelter and sat down next to a mother breast-feeding her baby. She was dead and the baby was alive."

"Did you take the baby?"

"Aminachka, how could I take the baby when I didn't know if I was going to be alive?"

Vladimir called and asked about my mother. I told him I missed him. He told me to buy the sticky buns from the bakery on the corner.

My mother told me she was starting to feel better. I didn't tell her her IV contained pulverized bees and that the pills she took four times a day were made of shark cartilage, or that the patients who had multiple sclerosis were given the same. The doctor believed they got sick from their car's catalytic converter.

At night I walked my mother to the large room across the hall where I would give her a bath. It was getting easier for her to get in and out of the deep tub.

She had been in the hospital for ten days, and I came in the morning and she looked pale.

"Amine, this German doctor told me, next time, I should come to him sooner. What? Does he believe we live more than once? I want to leave."

That afternoon she and I walked down the corridor. When we came to the window at the end, my mother leaned against the sill and looked out to the bare branches of the poplar trees.

"Is it possible that I won't see another spring?"

Phillip arranged for a car service to pick us up from JFK. We arrived late at night. The driver carried my mother up the stone steps.

"Leave me on the couch. I'll go upstairs in the morning."

I ordered a hospital bed, and a nurse from the hospice came every other day for a few hours. My mother signed a paper stating no extraordinary means should be used.

Warm Soft Cloth

Vladimir told me I had to start giving my mother coffee enemas. I asked him if he could come to see me. He didn't think it was a good idea. I told him no one would know. He said he couldn't. I told him if it wasn't for him, I wouldn't be able to get through this, and he said I was getting through this in spite of him.

"You told me, remember, when I called you from the airport before my mother and I went to Germany? Remember what you said? My mother will play with our child? What did you mean?"

"Exactly that."

"What?"

"You and I will have a child together."

"That's not possible. I had my tubes tied."

"Darling, everything can be undone. See if she will take the enemas. She has to get well."

———

Phillip was recruited by a multinational company that needed his expertise, and he left the firm he'd been with for twenty-five years. He said he would be making more money, and it was the right career move to make.

I drove Charlotte to swim practice every afternoon, and while I was gone, Stephen came up to the attic to be with his grandmother. He set up a Lego city by her bed. He didn't want to swim anymore. Michael was taking art as an elective and wanted to go to Spain for his junior year. Katherine was ranked fifth in the Northeast. March was very cold that year.

"Aminachka, my mother's maiden name was Borodina. Write it down, spell it the way you want to."

I got up from the wing chair that had stood downstairs by the fireplace in the center hall.

"Don't go, you'll remember. Sit with me. I want you to burn me . . . I don't know where. . . ."

"Do you want me to take you to Nantucket?"

"No. The water frightens me."

"To Nyack? To Hook Mountain?"

"No."

"Mama. Do you want to be with me? And when I go, we'll be together?"

She nodded and kept turning the amethyst ring on her middle finger. "I know how upset you will be when I die," and she started to cry.

"Mama, you're not going to die."

"Oey, Amine."

She had stopped coloring her hair—it was coming in white. I told her I'd do it for her. She said she didn't want me to handle the chemicals, that was what probably got her sick.

On her bedside table stood a jar of rich face cream, and under her pillows she kept a small icon in a gold frame that had belonged to her grandmother. She kept her nails short. I'd hand her a soft, warm cloth, and she would push back her cuticles.

"Aminachka, thank you for taking care of me."

"It's okay, Mom."

She told me she felt uneasy, she couldn't get comfortable. I called the nurse, and the doctor prescribed a morphine patch.

I called Natalie, and she flew in from San Francisco. She did jin shin on our mother, holding her opposite toes and fingers. I brought up the ironing board and ironed linen napkins while she slept.

I woke up at three and was going up the attic stairs just as Natalie was coming down to get me. Phillip came up and sat on the edge of one of the couches, his hands clasped, his head down. Natalie and I stood on either side of the bed and kept telling her it was all right, it was okay. At five in the morning, on Vladimir's birthday, she died. Natalie let go of her hand, turning around to prepare some Bach flower remedies she said would ease our mother's passage.

My right hand remained on my mother's forehead, and my left hand held her left hand. I felt an electrical shock pass up my right arm and go into my chest. I started to shake, and my ears started ringing, but I didn't let go. When it left, I let go of her hand and walked over to Phillip. He stood up from the couch and put his arms around me.

"I'm sorry. She was a wonderful woman."

I went downstairs to call my father to tell him my mother had died. I hadn't talked to him in ten years.

"Amine, I loved her. May—"

"I have to go."

Phillip was knotting his tie when I came in.

"Something happened."

"What?"

"No, it's okay, Phillip, nothing. It's just that I felt this—"

"I would stay, but you know I've got to go to work. It's my first day. Amine?"

"No, it's okay, I'm fine."

"I gave you my new number. You call me, okay?"

On Sunday I had people over. I introduced Vladimir to Phillip as my mother's doctor. They shook hands and said how pleased they were to meet.

Busy

Sarah wanted me to go with her to the St. Petersburg Film Festival for eight days; she had selected the American films that were to be shown. I would go as her assistant, and all expenses would be paid, except airfare. If we flew Aeroflot, we'd get a discount.

"When are you going?" Vladimir asked when I called him.

"The seventh of June."

"Beautiful. You'll be there for the White Nights."

"Wouldn't it be wonderful if you came with me?"

"How can I, darling? I have patients relying on me. Will I see you before you leave?"

"Can you see me?"

"Yes."

I had only talked to him on the phone since my mother died.

I packed one carry-on bag and asked Phillip if I could borrow his Leica.

"No."

"Why?"

"You'll either lose it, or it'll get stolen in that country. How are you getting to the airport?"

"I'm taking the train in, and then Sarah and I are taking a cab to JFK."

I saw Vladimir in the morning, before meeting Sarah at the airport.

"You don't have a camera with you."

"No."

"Why?"

"I don't have one."

"Take mine."

"I can't. It's a Leica."

"So what?"

"I'll either lose it, or it'll get stolen."

"Then we'll celebrate. Take it. Take a lot of pictures. We'll look at them when you get back. You'll show them in a gallery downtown. Have a wonderful time. I just hope you will want to come back. I want you to call me collect. Don't argue. I'll miss not hearing your voice. I love you."

"Vladimir, can we—"

"Let's wait."

Sarah and I stayed at the Astoria in St. Petersburg, the hotel where Hitler planned to have his victory party. We hardly slept. We saw films, went to receptions. I met Boris, a cabdriver, orphaned in the war. He took me to a church, and we lit candles for his parents and my mother. He wouldn't let me pay him. "Leningrad is my city." His ashtray was a soup can cut in half tied to the dashboard by wire. I left him a carton of Marlboros. He left a bouquet of red roses for me with the doorman. A film director showed us an empty basement and told us it was the Stray Dog Cabaret, where Akhmatova and Mayakovsky read their works. There were plans to restore it. We toured Pushkin's house. We took a hydroplane to the summer palaces of the royal family.

I called Vladimir.

"I went alone to the Neva this morning and watched the bridges go up. I saw couples kissing, and I kept thinking why aren't you here with me, why aren't we together?"

"We will be, darling. You'll see. We have the rest of our lives to be happy."

"When will I see you?"

"I'll be at the airport waiting for you."

I called Phillip and asked him how everyone was. He said everyone was fine. I told him how beautiful St. Petersburg was, and he said Russia had its problems and asked if I needed a car to pick me up from the airport. I told him Sarah's father had invited us to dinner. And that if it got too late, I'd spend the night at Sarah's and take the early morning train back.

Vladimir met me at the airport, and we took a cab into Manhattan. We had dinner at an Indian restaurant, and while having ice cream, he told me he had to see a patient in the hospital. He handed me a hundred-dollar bill to take a car home. I gave it back to him and took the train.

I met him weeks later for a walk in Central Park. I asked him to tell me again why we haven't been together. He again said we had to be careful, Phillip could not know about us. It would be disastrous for his health. We had to wait, and I had to learn patience. I told him to tell me our relationship was no longer possible. He said he couldn't. He wanted me. I told him I'd wait.

We watched a polar bear move back and forth through the water between two boulders. His fur was covered in yellow spots, and his belly was brown.

I started gaining weight. I told Carole I thought I should start seeing someone. She thought I meant a man. I told her I meant a psychiatrist. She told me not one of them could help me; they were crazy themselves.

Katherine was the only one who went to Nantucket that summer. She stayed at the house with Natalie and some friends from school.

Natalie told me she had started keeping a journal. She would write five pages every morning before she did anything else.

"I empty out my thoughts. Once I put them down, I don't go back to them. And no one else reads them either. Why don't you try doing it? It's helped me."

A few days later I received from her, in the mail, a blue cloth notebook.

The children started school. Soon Katherine would be going to Colorado to train.

"Mom, why don't you call me?"

"Katie darling, I'm sorry. I never know when to reach you. You're in class or on the mountain or the phone is busy."

"Pop gets through."

"That's good, darling."

"Mom, I miss you."

"I miss you too, baby."

"Can't you come up this weekend?"

"No, darling, I can't."

I waited for his phone call.

Michael went to Barcelona for a semester and started calling me Madre.

Charlotte was a sophomore in high school with a lot of friends, she begged for a private phone line. At recess Stephen played touch football and saw a special ed teacher for an hour every day to help his reading. Sarah and I kept reworking the script. Some of Phillip's clients stayed with his old firm, and he put in longer hours.

I started writing in the blue cloth notebook Natalie had sent me, and I started seeing a psychiatrist Sarah recommended.

Bird of Paradise

Dr. Roberta Blanc's office was in her apartment on West Ninth Street. She was in her early fifties and very heavy. She could barely walk—her shoes looked as if they were painted on. A small pastel portrait of her as a young woman hung in the entranceway. She was still beautiful. A message taped to the refrigerator read "Do Not Eat." She had a slight accent. She told me she was born in South Africa and that her parents were Belgian and escaped the Holocaust. Her father had associates in Capetown.

I told her my mother died, I had a lover although I never saw him, and I loved my children but I didn't care if a gorilla looked after them. I didn't think I loved my husband. Dr. Blanc asked if I thought I was in menopause.

I told her my mother made me wear undershirts even though I started growing breasts and the outline of my nipples could be seen. I was eleven. My friend's mother bought me a bra. I kept the bra hidden in the attic behind a loose brick of one of the chimneys. On a summer afternoon my mother came home before she said she would. I tried hiding. She pulled me out of the closet by my braid, hit my face with her fists, tore the bra off, and collapsed on the daybed in the kitchen, crying. I sat by her on the floor asking her to forgive me.

I told Dr. Blanc when I was six I couldn't go outside and I couldn't go to school. I had to stay in the apartment because my parents worked and there was no one to take care of me.

I told her when I was seven I stood on a stool to reach a jar of chocolate syrup kept on the top shelf of the cabinet. The jar fell and broke. I had to kneel in the corner with my arms in the air for a few hours. If I cried or if my arms went down, I was given something to hold—a book, a candlestick, a pail of not-too-much water, a crystal bowl.

I told her when I was eight my mother got tuberculosis. She went to a sanitarium in Rockland County to drink heavy cream, my father sold vacuum cleaners door to door, and I went to a children's home. On Sundays my father would visit me, but we couldn't visit my mother. She was contagious. My father took me to the apartment he was renting in Brooklyn. Our furniture was piled high in the living room. The bed was in the kitchen. He gave me a bath. After he laid me down, he put his tongue in my vagina and moved it around for a while.

I told her when I was thirteen my mother was out for the night visiting a friend, and my father caught me talking on the phone with a boy. He took his belt and beat me, holding the end without the buckle, until I bled.

My father told me my sister wasn't his. I locked myself in the bathroom and told him to go away. When he went to Mexico for the divorce, he brought back a leather bag, a hand-tooled bird of paradise splayed across the front, to hold my school books.

My father and mother were a handsome couple. My mother told me she never loved him, but I think that was after she found, in his pants pocket, an address written on a piece of paper above a blot of red lipstick. He told me he loved her; the other women meant nothing to him. On Sunday mornings he taught me to dance while my mother made pancakes. If anyone asked him for help, he would help them. He told me we were all brothers, that we were not to go through life spoiling the air. They went to dances every Saturday night in the winters. They danced beautifully. She wore a red carnation on the bodice of her black chiffon dress. He took me to the park and told me what he knew about the American Indians. He read Russian fairy tales to me and carried me on his shoulders. She smelled so good. He used apples to teach me arithmetic. She brushed and braided my hair and washed and ironed my dresses every day. He taught me how to drive a stick shift when I was thirteen. She'd sit on a blanket in the backyard soaking her feet in a white enamel basin filled with warm water and a floating half bar of Ivory soap. She painted her nails with Revlon's Snow Pink. She never wore stockings in the summer. He looked elegant in suits. When he left, she took a nurse's aide course and worked the four-to-midnight shift at the hospital. I came home from school and took care of Natalie. My mother never told me when she didn't have to go to work—I'd only find out after I came in and she wouldn't be in her uniform.

Dr. Blanc told me to close my eyes and envision my mother sitting in the chair over in front of the windows.

Do you see her? She's smiling at you. Wrap her...first...in white light...now pink...and now...golden...smile at her... she is still smiling...tell her you forgive her...now...let her go.

She didn't tell me what to do with my father.

One morning I came downstairs and couldn't find my blue cloth notebook. I asked, and no one knew where it was.

About a month later Dr. Blanc suggested seeing me with Phillip. She thought it would be helpful, but if I felt uncomfortable with that, then of course we wouldn't do it.

That night Phillip walked back into the kitchen as I was cleaning up.

"Amine."

"Um."

"May I talk to you?"

I stood up from washing the floor around the refrigerator that always seemed to be dirty, and we faced each other across the island.

"Amine, you've been a good wife to me."

"You haven't been a good husband to me." I avoided looking at him.

"I know. But that is going to change. I've seen Roberta. Amine, I want you to know I am going to dedicate the rest of my life to making you happy. Do you know you're more beautiful now than you have ever been? Do you know how much I love you? Amine, there has never been anyone else for me. I have never looked at another woman. I'm at fault. I know that. I'm going to change. I'm sorry."

The next day Phillip sent a large bouquet of flowers.

Phillip and I went to see Dr. Blanc.

"Amine, you and Phillip complement one another. You're softer, less complicated. Phillip is more focused, disciplined. The left side of his brain is more dominant, yours is the right. If you can make this marriage work, it's an ideal combination. Now, Phillip has something to say to you."

He had read my notebook. I wasn't to be upset, he blamed himself. This guy was not who I thought he was. He was a fraud. And the reason Phillip knew is because he hired a private investigator, and he pulled out from his breast pocket a folded sheet of paper. The New York authorities have complained about his holding himself out as a medical doctor. He has a dental degree and he has been with a woman for the past eighteen years. I stood up and said I had to go. Dr. Blanc sat silently by, looking at me. Phillip reached for my hand. He told me to stay. He loved me. As far as he was concerned, it never happened. He would never bring it up, ever. He forgave me. It had been his fault. He didn't want to lose me, he didn't want to lose his family. He would do anything to stay together. To please not to leave him.

I asked him why he had read my notebook. He told me he had found it on his chair in the kitchen.

After the session Phillip went to work, and I drove to Westchester. I was in bed in the middle of the afternoon when Phillip called. I was to stop crying. We had a wonderful family, and he would do everything and anything for me. He loved me, he had always loved me, and he would always love me.

We started seeing Dr. Blanc together. She said we had to come together on Katherine's skiing. It wasn't good for her to be getting crossed signals from us.

"Amine, Phillip is right. It would be good for her career."

Phillip stopped drinking. In my notebook he read that I thought a man needed to know just two things about a woman, dancing and what flowers to give. He brought me flowers every day. He told me he was working on a surprise for me. Our love-making started lasting hours every night and on Saturday and Sunday mornings. We started going out to dinner, sometimes even on weekdays.

"Amine, let's move back to the city." Phillip's face had become softer, and the ends of his mouth didn't go down as much. "Yes. Why not? Let's do it. You've always wanted to move."

"Maybe we should wait until Charlotte finishes high school."

"Why? Let's do it now. We can't buy an apartment right away. We'll rent for now and use the house on weekends. Or maybe later we'll sell the house and buy an apartment."

"I think it'll be too hard for Charlotte. All her friends are here."

"She'll get to see her friends. She's got to cut down on her socializing anyway. At the rate she's going, she'll be lucky if a second-rate college takes her. She'll be better off in a private school."

"What about Stephen's soccer?"

"He won't have to quit. The coach says there's no problem with Stephen remaining in the league. It just means it'll take longer getting him to his practices. It'll be great for them, for us. They'll be in private school. I'll be home earlier. Why don't you start looking for an apartment?"

I got my period and bled for days. I finally went to a gynecologist in Mount Kisco who told me I was anemic, and if the bleeding didn't subside after taking progesterone, I would most likely need a hysterectomy.

I took the progesterone and iron pills and felt sick. I stopped taking them and asked Phillip to get me red caviar at Zabar's on his way home. My mother had told me red caviar had all the iron you needed.

I asked Dr. Blanc to recommend a gynecologist. She told me before she gave me a name I should go to the jin shin practitioner who had worked on her husband before and after his open heart surgery. Her husband had made a complete recovery, and she knew jin shin had saved his life. I called Natalie, and she told me Dr. Blanc was right, Mary Sang was excellent. How many times did she tell me to start doing it?

I lay on a massage table in a small room of Mary Sang's apartment. The walls were padded and covered in raw silk. She asked me to take off my belt, and she covered me with a down blanket, and while Charlie Parker played softly, she placed her left palm on my coccyx and her right palm on my pubis, and I fell asleep.

I went to Mary every day for a week. The bleeding stopped after the third day. When I went back to the gynecologist in Mount Kisco a month later, he told me my uterus was normal and I was no longer anemic, but I needed to continue taking progesterone, and it wouldn't hurt if I continued with the iron pills as well.

Diana was now a partner in a real estate firm, and she took me to see a vacant seven-room apartment on West Eighty-Sixth Street. An opera singer had lived in it for fifty-five years. She had died in the spring, and her belongings were sent to her ninety-six-year-old cousin in Israel. The new owners of the building were planning on spending a hundred thousand dollars to renovate the apartment. They then could bring it out of rent control and into fair market value. She urged me to get it; even without price restrictions it was a steal.

"Amine, grab it. It may go co-op, and you'll be on the ground floor. Phillip told me he'll take anything you like. He's so in love with you."

When we were having coffee at French Roast, I told her about Vladimir.

"You're not involved with him now, are you?"

"No."

"Good."

Tested Negative

"Amine, I don't want to frighten you, but I got tested for AIDS, and I think you should do the same. By the way it was negative," Phillip told me when I called him from Sarah's to ask him what he wanted for dinner. I left Sarah's apartment, walked to a store that carried Godiva chocolates, and ate the contents of the box on the drive back to Westchester. I made dinner, did the driving back and forth to the pool and soccer practice, and went to bed. Phillip had a dinner meeting with clients.

I called Vladimir the next morning after Charlotte and Stephen left for school.

"I have to see you."

"I can't, not now."

"It's very important, please."

"Can you be here in an hour?"

"Yes."

"I'll meet you in the front. Have the doorman ring me, I'll come out."

It took me forty minutes to get into the city. I found a parking space on the street and walked to his building. He was outside waiting for me.

"I am in awe of you," he said as I came up to him. "You look magnificent. Let's walk." He took my hand. "How have you been?"

"Vladimir, Phillip knows about us." He stopped and looked at me.

"How?"

"I kept a notebook, and he found it."

"A notebook? You kept a notebook? Why did you do that? This is very bad. Do you know that you have just killed Phillip? I was so careful not to injure him in any way, and you disregarded all that I tried to do. Didn't I tell you we needed time? Do you know how hard it's been for me not to see or talk to you all this time? You have ruined it for us. I have to go."

"Please, let's talk."

"There's nothing to say." He turned and walked away.

After Charlotte realized we were serious about moving to New York, she stopped talking to me. She and Katherine went to Chile to train with Katherine's ski team. Katherine called and told us a U.S. Ski Team coach had said Charlotte should quit swimming and become a skier. Stephen was at camp in New Hampshire, the youngest camper ever to receive a ribbon in swimming. Michael was in training, biking sixty to a hundred miles a day. Sarah and I finished the script. Phillip lost a major client.

The apartment on West Eighty-Sixth Street was the size of the house on Sheppard Road without the attic and basement. The living room, dining room, kitchen, and maid's room faced the street, and the three bedrooms and baths faced the inner courtyard. The walls were two feet thick, and the ceilings were twelve feet high. The sun poured through the rooms. A group of businessmen had bought the building from a woman who had neglected it for years.

Phillip had them write in the contract to install a fireplace in the living room and an oak floor in the kitchen. I came in every day to see how the work was going, bringing coffee and something I baked for the construction men. All of them were from Serbia and understood Russian. I talked the foreman out of ordering the green and black marble for the master bath and showed him a piece of beige-pink limestone, convincing him it wasn't too porous. I didn't want a Jacuzzi, I wanted a deep English soaking tub. I didn't want the fixtures or the vanity mirror. I wanted the same French brass fixtures that were in Sheppard Road and the five-by-ten-foot mirror framed in walnut I'd seen in an antique shop on Greenwich Avenue.

"Who the hell does that woman think she is?" I was told was said after everything I wanted was ordered, delivered, and installed.

Carole called to tell me she was running a tag sale for a woman whose husband left her.

"You're nuts if you don't buy it. She told me he paid fifteen thousand for it, and I told her she won't get anything even close to that. Especially in July. Anyway, she can't stand him, and she wants to get rid of everything that reminds her of him. I told her if she's serious in selling it, she's got to go way down in price. I'd buy it, but I already have one plus my fox. It looks great on you."

"Carole, what do I need a mink coat for?"

"No, of course not. You don't need anything except that drug dealer jacket of yours."

"It's warm."

"You look horrible in it. It has too many pockets. Don't you think it's about time you got yourself something real?"

I bought a blue and white platter, twelve crystal glasses, and linen napkins.

"If she doesn't know they're Baccarat, I'm not going to tell her. Take all the linen."

That night Carole walked over with the mink coat on a hanger over her arm.

"Jesus, don't you people believe in lights? I almost fell getting over here. Where's Phillip?"

"He's upstairs."

"Put the coat on. I know he'll buy it once he sees you in it. He can afford it." Carole took the mink coat off the padded ivory-velvet hanger, draped it over my shoulders, and pushed me toward the staircase. Phillip was in bed reading and watching TV.

"Phillip, look at Amine. She has on a twenty-thousand-dollar mink coat. I can get it for eight hundred."

Phillip looked up and smiled. I walked between the antique French cherry table that the TV rested on and the four-poster bed.

"Put it on," Phillip said. I pulled my arms through the sleeves of the mink coat. "It really looks wonderful on you. Do you want it?"

"Does it really look good on me?"

"Yes. I want you to have it."

Svetlana was visiting from Moscow—I met her through friends. She was seventy-eight and taught character dance at the Bolshoi Ballet. When she told me she didn't know how she was going to get through another Russian winter, I gave her the mink coat.

A week later, on a Sunday morning, I had just come back from buying the paper and bagels.

"Where's the mink coat?"

"Mink coat?"

"Yeah, mink coat. Where is it?"

"It's upstairs."

"It's not in the closet. Where is it?"

"It should be in the closet."

"Amine, where's the coat?"

"I think I brought it to the apartment and put it in the cedar closet."

"Bullshit. That apartment is all torn up. Who has it? I want it back. I'm telling you, I want it hanging in the closet upstairs by to-morrow night."

I went upstairs and called Carole from Charlotte's room.

"Carole, can I borrow your mink coat?"

"Why?"

"I need it just for a few days. Please."

"Why?"

"I gave the mink coat to Svetlana, and Phillip just found out, and he wants it back."

"You are kidding me. You'd better get it back. What does an eighty-year-old need with a mink coat? And in Russia where they don't know mink from muskrat. You have got to be locked up. Do you know you gave away a twenty-five-thousand-dollar coat? What is wrong with you?"

"Let me borrow your coat."

"I'm not taking my valuable coat out of storage so you can— wait a second, why wasn't your mink in storage?"

"I was going to do it. Carole, just let me borrow the coat."

"No. So it can hang in your closet and be eaten by moths? You had no business giving that coat away."

"Carole, I need the coat for one night. I just need Phillip to see it."

"No, I won't. You are so . . . Phillip gave it to you, and he has every right to be angry."

"Can't I do what I want with my gifts?"

"No."

Svetlana was staying with her sister in Brooklyn. I drove there the next day.

Without a word she went to the closet and took the mink coat out from its protective wrap and gave it to me. She told me not to be upset, that things always turn out the way they're supposed to.

I brought the mink coat back and hung it in the closet.

In August Phillip had to go to Russia to meet with clients, and I went to Moscow and St. Petersburg with him. We stayed in five-star hotels, went to museums, walked through parks, visited palaces, and made love in rooms looking out to a river, a cathedral. Phillip bought me a wool scarf of woven red poppies, a Paleh box of a woman standing in a forest, six dinner plates rimmed in gold, each with a different Fabergé egg painted in the center, and a replica of a small bronze horse said to have belonged to Cleopatra, from the Hermitage gift shop.

When Charlotte came back from Chile, she quit swimming. Katherine and Michael drove back to school, Stephen started playing goalie, and I began packing for West Eighty-Sixth Street.

I didn't get tested for AIDS.

High Ceilings

Phillip decided we couldn't afford to use Sheppard Road as a weekend house, and it was rented to an executive, his wife, and their two daughters. They had no pets, or so they told us. They had bought an acre in the new development off Mayfair Lane, and their house would take about a year to build.

I didn't want to leave anything behind, and while walking up the stairs from the laundry room to the kitchen, I noticed something lying on the top shelf, above the dryer.

It was Katherine's notebook from freshman year. The English assignment was to write the background of a country-western song.

Looking back at it now I regret meeting him. Although we had three lovely children together, his lack of acknowledgment to-wards me was enough to drive a person insane. I was young and naïve and had no sense of myself when I made the decision to marry. It's not that he beat me or treated me badly; just the fact that in his eyes I was just a shadow chilled me inside and all the love I had for him. Now that I am on my own I have more sense of myself. Even though the pay is lousy and I hardly get to see my kids I had the strength to leave him. But was losing all that worth just to regain my strength. That is something I must ask myself and never know the answer. All I know is that I will never go back.

Then a few pages later:

I know that I will not become a housewife in my later years. During my childhood my mother has always done everything for her children. I see her as an angel because I could never do what she does so well. It's too agonizing. Hopefully after college I will be able to support myself on my own. I do not want to feel dependent on someone.

I hid the notebook.

Carole came over for a cup of tea.

"I have to tell you again, your moving to New York is one of the dumbest things I have ever heard. You're ruining your children's lives. I cannot believe you're dragging them into that sewer. This has got to be your idea. Phillip can't be that stupid."

"It was Phillip's idea."

"Well, I can't understand any of it."

"You'll come visit me?"

"I can't believe you're leaving."

The Harvey Brothers moved us from Sheppard Road to West Eighty-Sixth Street a week before school started. Charlotte was a junior in a private school on Central Park West. Stephen was a fifth-grader in a private school on the Upper East Side.

Charlotte was not happy. Phillip bought her a TV for her room and a phone with her own unlisted number. She'd watch MTV, listen to her CDs, eat Häagen-Dazs Double Chocolate Fudge, and stay on the phone with her friends in Westchester.

She and I walked to a hardware store on Amsterdam Avenue to buy picture hooks. She wanted to cover the walls of her room with framed photographs of her friends.

"It's so dirty. I can't believe we live here. I hate this place."

"Sweetheart, the city is going to be so good for you. You will have such a lovely time here. Everything you could possibly want is here. You'll see—once you make friends here, you will have a great time."

"Mom, do you know you are a fucking piece of shit?"

I smiled.

"Did you hear me? You are a fucking piece of shit."

"What do you want me to say to that, Charlotte?"

"Why don't you hit me?" And she started to cry.

Stephen became friends with three of his classmates, and they'd rollerblade around the courtyard, and after one of the tenants complained, they met in our apartment. Padded in ice hockey gear bought at the school's annual used sports equipment sale, they'd slam into each other.

Molly and I went to Central Park early in the mornings, before the police issued tickets to owners of unleashed dogs. I'd leave the park at West Seventy-second Street and shop for dinner along Broadway. I'd stand in the courtyard and listen to stories about people who used to live in the building.

Luis, one of the doormen, said he'd teach Diana and me the salsa. We met at the Latin Quarter, and the three of us danced till four to a live band.

If Stephen didn't have friends over or if he wasn't on his skateboard or rehearsing for the musical his class was putting on, he and I would take long walks. If it rained, we'd go to a movie.

Phillip brought flowers once a week and started drinking one glass of white wine after coming home from work. We stopped seeing Dr. Blanc. Phillip got tickets to *Miss Saigon*. We went to a restaurant on Broadway that made good hamburgers. Charlotte and I joined a gym. Phillip started playing the piano again. Michael was in his last year of college. Katherine was in France, skiing.

Phillip and Stephen took the crosstown bus every morning to Stephen's school. Charlotte walked the few blocks to hers, and I'd meet Diana for coffee after Molly and I had been in Central Park and Diana had taken her morning ballet class. Diana had married Will, an investment banker, after divorcing David. When their twin boys were born, they moved from Will's Riverside Drive apartment to a fourteen-room co-op on Central Park West. Diana's older daughter was in Paris, studying fashion, and her younger daughter was a bartender in the city. David died of a brain tumor a few years after he left Diana.

Dentures

"Diana, I have to tell you about a dream I had last night. It was so real. I was in an amphitheater sitting close to a body wrapped in a white shroud lying on a table; the head was detached, and a priest was massaging the face. False teeth came out and he laid the teeth beside the head. Lots and lots of people, and we're all watching. The body's your uncle but not your uncle, you know? Your aunt comes over, holding a basin, and she asks me to take a small piece of the heart. And the heart is in pieces. I see it in the bowl. I know it's part of the ritual, and I put a small piece in my mouth. I can actually feel the graininess of it and I can't swallow it. Your aunt says, 'No, my dear, you have to have it with dates,' and she gives me three dates, and I can actually taste their sweetness, and I eat the heart, and I think to myself what a lovely way to say good-bye. I run to your mother—I've never seen her before but I know she is your mother—and I tell her, 'Diana should be here,' and your mother says, 'Diana knows her father is dead. She knows where we are, and if she wants to be here, she will.' Your uncle turned into your father. Diana, I felt the heart in my mouth. It was so real. Diana. I was with Vladimir once. I was so close to coming, and I just stopped. I was afraid I was going to kill him if I came."

"Amine, why don't you see a therapist? I know somebody who's very good."

"Maybe. Is it a he or a she?"

"His name is Alan. I have his number at the office. I'll phone you with it. Will's coming back Monday."

"Why didn't you go to Singapore with him?"

"I've got too much going on here. You should sell the Westchester house and buy an apartment. Everyone keeps saying things just can't keep going up. But I know . . . Amine? Come on."

"What?"

"You're tuning out. You know, it's not easy being with you when you get like that. Phillip called me at my office yesterday. He asked me if I could tell him what would make you happy. Amine, you've got to try. Listen, you know I've been through it, when David left . . . anyway, I sympathize with Phillip."

"I think I'm going to start seeing Mary Sang again."

"You should see Alan."

"I was thinking maybe I should go back to school. I barely got through high school. Maybe if I started again."

I went to Mary Sang twice a week. I'd lie on the table in the silk room, she would put her hands on me, and I would talk. She told me a client of hers—she wouldn't give me her name—talked about a doctor who sounded very much like Vladimir. She hesitated telling me, she knew it was unethical, but then she decided I needed to know.

It was Phillip's and my twenty-fifth wedding anniversary. We went to St. John for a long weekend. Our bungalow was at the water's edge. A wooden fan spun above the bed, and from the open windows the sweet smell of the tropics swept through the room. Each night a different-colored seashell appeared on our pillows with two small pieces of milk chocolate wrapped in gold foil. We walked to a beach where I swam naked while Phillip sat, wearing his trunks, on one of the bungalow's queen-size bath sheets looking out beyond me and the moored sailboats to the faint outline of St. Croix. We took a day sail with a gay skipper. Anchored in a green water cove, we ate tuna and mango salad and drank rum ice tea. On our third day, the sitter called and told us the pediatrician suspected Stephen had Lyme disease, after Stephen complained of a headache and couldn't walk. We flew back that day. As soon as Stephen was put on antibiotics, the pain in his legs went away. I made him eat a lot of yogurt.

Phillip had to go to London for a few days, and he wanted me to go with him.

We stayed at a small hotel near the Victoria and Albert Museum. The room faced an inner garden. The weather was warm for February, and I would have afternoon tea in one of the two public rooms downstairs, waiting for Phillip to be finished with his meetings.

I criticized him for his jogging style when we ran through Hyde Park. In the afternoon he bought me a brown leather briefcase.

He hired a car and a driver to take us to Bath to see the Roman ruins. He bought me a silver tea set and a cashmere sweater. After exchanging the sweater for a scarf, he took me to a French-Vietnamese restaurant. The silver chopsticks kept making a noise against the black glass plates. He sent the wine back.

"Amine, I love you."

Svetlana's sister got ill, and Svetlana postponed going back to Moscow indefinitely. I'd take the subway to Brooklyn, and the three of us would sit in the kitchen and have tea. They'd remember their childhood. They lived in Moscow, and their father was a professor of mathematics. "How he loved us, and how we loved him." When Svetlana's sister went into the bedroom to lie down, I'd talk to Svetlana about Vladimir. She told me they called my years the Balzac years. I asked her what she meant? A woman over forty looking for trouble. Did she really think that that was what I was doing? A little, she said, and she bit into a biscuit and broke her upper bridge. I called Vladimir.

"How have you been?"

"We moved to New York. We're trying to make it work."

"I hope you succeed."

"I have a friend who needs work done on her teeth."

"Let her come in to see me. I've moved to a new office on Park Avenue."

"I know."

"You were here?"

"I drove by last night."

I spoke to him again a few days later.

"Amine, your friend Svetlana called. She told me she has five teeth left."

"Yes?"

"She asked if I could do anything for her."

"Can you?"

"Of course. I use a laboratory in Switzerland. Our Svetlana will have the most exquisite teeth. Come with her to my office."

"When?"

"Tomorrow at two."

He called me into the office. Svetlana was in the chair, her hand on her jaw. He told me she had to heal first before he took an impression. Svetlana's sister gave me two thousand dollars to give Vladimir. If he needed more, she would pay him a little each month.

Svetlana came down with a fever, and she wouldn't take the antibiotics he had given her. He didn't return my calls. I took Svetlana to a dentist whom Dr. Weiss in 5B recommended. The dentist told me she had an infection and gave me a prescription for an antibiotic that she took. He took an impression and extracted the three teeth left on the bottom. He made a temporary set of dentures, to keep the swelling down. After she healed, he would make a permanent set, and he would need to see her again. I set up a payment schedule with his secretary.

A few mornings later I stood behind a tree across from Vladimir's office and waited for him. As he unlocked his door, I crossed Park Avenue. He was taking off his coat when I came in.

I asked him if he had received my messages. He told me he had to go out of town on an emergency. I told him I had to take Svetlana to a dentist and I had to pay this dentist, and could I have some of the money back that Svetlana's sister had given him?

He told me he couldn't. He'd paid for the dentures when they arrived from Switzerland. They cost more than two thousand dollars. I asked him how much more, and he said he couldn't remember, and I asked him if he could give me the dentures and I would pay him the difference, whatever it was. He told me he couldn't keep the dentures in his office, there wasn't any room. They were in his apartment, and he would send them to me.

I called Carole that evening.

"Carole, I have to sell the mink coat."

"Why?"

"Carole, can you please buy it back?"

"How much did you pay me for it?"

"Eight hundred."

"Why do you need the money?"

"I've got to do something with it."

"Like what?"

"Carole, you know my blue and white platter?"

"Which one?"

"The one with the seashells and battle scene."

"You want to sell it?"

"Yes."

"What did you pay for it?"

"A thousand."

"Okay. Why do you need the money?"

"I want to buy a Chanel bag."

"Yeah, right. If that were only true."

Inconvenienced

Charlotte hated her school, the students. She wouldn't participate in any after-school activity. She would walk to the apartment after her last class and go to her room to do her homework. She'd tell Stephen to go to the corner store and get her some candy. She started getting straight A's. Her science teacher recommended her for a seminar run by Wellesley College. She didn't go. Friday afternoons, as soon as school was out, she'd take the car and drive to Westchester to be with her friends. She'd come home Sunday night. In the spring she decided to go back to swimming. She barely spoke to me.

Stephen would be going to camp for his third summer. Charlotte would be a lifeguard at the Westchester Country Club and stay with her friend Julie. Katherine would be on Nantucket, cleaning cars for Hertz and living in the house with Natalie. Michael would be cycling and going to races.

———————

I took Stephen to Paragon Sports to buy what he needed for camp. Phillip returned early from work and sat at the dining-room table beside Stephen. He changed out of his suit into shorts and a T-shirt.

When I brought Phillip his dinner, he said he didn't want it—he would have it later, and he would fix it himself. He asked what we had bought. Stephen, in his hurry to leave the table, overturned his glass of milk. He wiped it up with a white linen napkin and went to his room to get the hiking boots.

"Why hiking boots?" Phillip asked. "You'll never wear them. No one wears hiking boots." He lifted them. "They're too heavy. Why did you get hiking boots for him? You have no conception of money. Throw it away. He won't wear them. No one wears hiking boots." He put the hiking boots on the table and picked up a half-empty glass of wine. I took the hiking boots off the table and put them on the floor beside his bare feet.

Stephen left the table and went into his room. I began eating the chicken he had left on his plate. Stephen came back and showed Phillip a picture of himself standing on the top of Mount Washington with a group of boys.

Phillip pointed to the one boy who wasn't wearing hiking boots.

"His feet hurt him the whole time," said Stephen.

"Why don't you stop drinking?"

"Don't talk to me." Phillip refilled his glass. "Wine is good for me—it lowers my cholesterol. It's good for my heart. Look at you. You're at least thirty pounds overweight. What's that doing to your heart?" Stephen picked up the hiking boots and photograph and went to his room.

On a late June morning Phillip, Charlotte, and I drove to Poughkeepsie.

It was the tenth heat; Charlotte was swimming the fifty-meter fly in the fourteenth heat. Phillip was standing beside me. A woman sat under a green-and-white-striped canopy nearby. It was painful to look at her face; her nose was red and puffy. Over-exposure to the sun? Too much drinking? Both? Her hair was dyed brownish red, she wore white slip-on canvas shoes, and the top three buttons of her black cotton shirt were unbuttoned, exposing a small diamond on a thin gold chain. She kept glancing at the heat sheet, talking to the woman beside her. How are the children doing? Isn't this some weather? Costco was selling flats of bego-nias for five dollars. I imagined her life. What did she do during the day to make her finally go to sleep? She was married, I saw her ring. Did they still make love? Was it satisfying for them both? Was there anything left of his want, or was it all released?

It was the thirteenth heat—Charlotte was up next. Her cap was on, and she was adjusting her goggles. A minute later she won. It was her seventeenth birthday.

I remembered the morning she was born. The nurse told me I was hardly dilated and should have stayed home. She told me to walk the corridor, and when I felt a contraction coming on, I was to press my hands against the wall and bear down as hard as I could. That would get me started. I walked the corridor once and told Phillip I had to lie down. The nurse saw me from her station and in her Irish brogue yelled out I was a lazy one. Phillip yelled back for her to come quick. There wasn't enough time to call the doctor, and she delivered Charlotte. "She's going to be a lucky one," she said when Charlotte came out in a translucent membrane. She told me fishermen in Ireland pay dearly for the sac; it meant they'd return home safe, with a lot of fish. She asked if she could keep it.

Charlotte won the one-hundred- and two-hundred-meter butterfly, and we drove back to the city. We parked the car in the garage and walked to a Mexican restaurant to celebrate her birth-day. She asked Phillip if she could taste his margarita.

"We've been sitting here and the people next to us are already getting theirs. This is ridiculous."

"Pop, they can hear you. Calm down."

"I will not calm down." He called the waitress.

"I'm sorry, sir. It's because your daughter ordered the appetizer and you and your wife didn't. That delayed your order. I'm sorry."

"That is the stupidest excuse I have ever heard. I'm telling you, if we don't get our food in two minutes, we're leaving."

"I'm terribly sorry, sir. I'll go into the kitchen and find out what's holding up your order."

"Pop, please, it's my birthday. Let's try to have a good time."

"Phillip, what is the big fucking deal?"

"The big fucking deal is I'm hungry, and I am not letting this go on anymore."

Charlotte left.

"Since you're so hungry, you can have mine too when it comes."

I caught up with Charlotte on Eighty-Fifth Street.

"Leave me alone. I hate the both of you."

I was in bed when Phillip walked in an hour later.

"You've phoned him three times."

Calls within New York City, I later found out, are not individually shown on the monthly statement, but an itemized calling sheet can be sent upon the request of the customer.

"I called him because he did some work for Svetlana."

"You're a liar, and you and I are finished."

"Phillip, I called him because I couldn't get in touch with him any other way. Listen to me."

"I'm through listening to you. We're finished. You had me shake that creep's hand. I have your diary with someone I trust. I've attached a handwritten letter that if anything should happen to me—"

"Happen to you, like what?"

"You know."

"No, I don't know, tell me. Oh. That's right, Phillip. If anything should happen to you, I'll get all your money. You'd better change your will so I don't get any of it."

"I have."

"You have?"

"Get out."

"Why don't you."

"I'm not getting out. I'm not the one who's going to be incon-venienced. You're the one who's getting out. Go to your lover. Let him support you."

I moved to the maid's room off the kitchen. The table by my side of the bed on which Phillip left twenty or forty dollars every morning before going to work remained.

Do You Want to Make Her Happy?

You could get twenty dollars an hour cleaning houses on Nantucket. I didn't tell anyone I was going to do it, just going to Nantucket earlier than planned. Phillip said he'd let me know in advance if he decided to fly in.

Katherine was waiting for me on the dock as the ferry approached. She stood with Molly beside the Beast, the name she gave the Jeep Wagoneer we kept on the island. Her hair always got lighter in the summer. She wore one of the beaded necklaces she made. At the end of August she was going to Europe with two other skiers and Doug Wilde, a ski coach, to train for the Europa Cup. She was postponing going to Dartmouth for a year.

We got to the house. Katherine brought my bag up to my room, and as I was making tea, she told me she didn't want to go to France. It was all she had been thinking about since she arrived on the island. She didn't want to ski anymore. She wanted to go to school and graduate with her class. If the U.S. Ski Team took her, it would mean a two-year commitment at least, and she wouldn't want to go to college after that.

"Katie, if you want to go to college now, go."

"Mom, what's Pop going to say?"

"Who gives a shit what he says?"

"Mom."

"Katie, I don't care. Skiing is dangerous. It's worse if your heart's not in it. If you got injured, and I knew you didn't want to ski, how do you think I'd feel? No, Katie, you're not doing it anymore."

Dartmouth wanted a letter stating why she had changed her mind. She wrote the letter and FedExed it the same day she called her father.

Phillip asked to speak to me.

"You put her up to this. You are really a menace. She is making the biggest mistake of her life."

"Phillip, she does not want to ski."

"No. It's you who doesn't want her to ski. You never supported her. You call yourself a mother? Does a mother bring her children down because she hasn't done anything with her own life? Listen, I see résumés all the time, and if I saw one that looked like Katherine's, I'd grab her."

"She doesn't want to ski anymore."

"She has to. She can write her own ticket anywhere after this. Amine, you're supporting me on this."

"I am not."

Katherine told me she had a dream that she stopped skiing and her father stopped talking to her. I told her that could never happen. He might be angry for a while, but he'd get over it. What could he do? Force her? He loved her, and she loved him, and that could never change. She had to make her own decisions, and she was not to do what other people wanted her to do, especially her mother and father.

"Do you remember, Katie, you were fourteen and it was summer and we were here on Nantucket and you wanted to go out with your friends at night and you asked me when you had to be home? And I told you you could be home when you wanted to be home. Why do you think I said that? I wanted you to decide for yourself when to come back. I didn't want you looking at the clock—worrying. I grew up ... it doesn't matter. Everything will be fine."

"There's no money to send her to college."

"Phillip, you find the money to send her. If you can pay Wilde and for everything else, you can send your daughter to college."

"Doug and I had an agreement on how he was to be paid."

"He was still going to have to be paid. Right? You call Dartmouth and arrange a payment schedule with them."

"She's letting Doug down. He's going to have to scratch the whole thing."

"Why? Wilde has the other two girls."

"We were the only ones paying him."

I went to the real estate offices in town and told them I needed work. I started immediately. I brought my own cleaning supplies. I did only rentals, two houses a day, three to four hours in each house. I made eight hundred dollars a week. I'd clean before the renters arrived and after they left. If the renters stayed for more than a week, I'd sometimes be asked to clean while they were there.

"Amine, would you mind ironing? I have a thing with cotton napkins. I brought my napkins on vacation, can you believe that? I'll pay you extra."

"No, that's fine. I like to iron."

I usually biked to my jobs, but when the houses were far away, I asked Katherine to drive me. I wanted her to come in and see the view from the master bedroom terrace of a house out in Tom Nevers. She wouldn't. She said it was too upsetting for her, that it was hard enough driving me to my jobs.

"You better watch what you say to me. You're not making me feel ashamed of what I'm doing. I have to make money. I want you to go to the health food store and get me a bottle of Citrisolve, a large bottle, and when you get back, I want you in this house, and I want you to look at the view."

"Mom, Citrisolve is expensive."

"I don't give a flying fuck. And don't you tell me. I'm through explaining why I want something. I told you to do it. You do it. Now. Ashamed? Don't you ever say that to me again."

"Mom, I didn't say I was ashamed of you. I'm sorry."

"Okay."

"I love you, Mom. I'll be back soon."

Geraldine invited me to the party she was giving to help Kenneth Bradshaw get reelected, and she asked me to bring the tamari–maple syrup–nut mix I make.

"Why Amine, what are you doing here?" asked Felicity Grant, who rented her house on Cliff Road and hired me for every other Thursday morning.

"Geraldine is my neighbor."

"Do you own a house on Eel Point Road?"

"Several."

"Gee, maybe you should be paying me."

I smiled.

Stephen and his friend, Sam, sold chocolate chip cookies on the beach. In the morning they'd bike to town to buy the ingredients.

I told them to use Rémy Martin instead of vanilla, to use less flour and more butter, and not to worry if they came out soft. They'd be in the cooler, and people would be eating them right away.

"You're to always say thank you, and you are never, never to insist. And both of you look very handsome."

Either Katherine or Natalie would drive the boys to Surfside or Nobadeer. Stephen and Sam would then each grab an end of the cooler. With hand-painted signs saying "Do you want to make her happy? Buy her a cookie" taped to each side, they walked up and down the beach. By two in the afternoon they had usually made a seventy-dollar profit. They'd go body surfing, their money, secured within a rubber band, inside the empty cooler.

Sam invited Stephen to Montreal to visit his grandparents— their house was on a lake. They were thinking of pooling their money and buying a used Zodiac with a twenty-five-horsepower motor. The boys took the ferry. Sam's parents met them in Hyannis, and they drove to Canada. They'd be back a few days before school started.

Katherine left for Manhattan to get ready for college. Phillip was to drive her to New Hampshire. I would stay in Nantucket for another week, and Natalie would stay the winter. We had to get another wood-burning stove. Ours had cracked when someone put a log on the top of it and used an ax to splinter the log into kindling. Natalie was going to see if she could pick one up cheap. I told her to order one from Vermont Castings and I'd pay for it.

Katherine called me on the evening Phillip drove her to school.

"Mom."

"Hi. You're there already?"

"Mom, I know everything."

"What do you know?"

"I know that you were with a scumbag and that if Pop hadn't moved to the city, you would have left us."

"Katie?"

"How could you do it?"

"What's the name of your dorm?"

She hung up.

Natalie gave me her credit card to fly to Boston and rent a car. Katherine was sharing a room with another girl who hadn't arrived yet. She was on her computer when I walked in. I sat on her bed.

"Katie, this doesn't concern you. What concerns you are your studies and your own life."

"My life is over."

"Katie, your life is not over. You are at a great college. You're going to take interesting courses. You're going to make a lot of friends, and you're on the ski team, and you're one of the best athletes they have."

"Don't talk to me about skiing. You never wanted me to ski. Do you know how I feel? I can't look at you. I don't want to be with you. How could you do it? I knew something was wrong when you hardly came to see me. It sickens me when I think of you with that guy. I want to kill him. How could you do this to us? Why don't you leave like you were planning to do?"

I drove back to Boston, turned the car in with a full tank, took a bus to Hyannis, walked the three blocks to the dock, took the passenger ferry to Nantucket, and finished the few houses I had left to clean.

A week later I got to the New York apartment late at night and woke Phillip.

"I want you to tell me why you told Katie."

"Because my therapist told me to."

"You've been seeing a therapist? Since when?"

"Since you started fucking that guy."

"Why did you tell her?"

"I told you why."

"I don't understand. Explain it to me."

"He told me to tell them because he didn't want them to think it was their fault."

"The other children know?"

"I haven't told Stephen."

"Jesus, Phillip. You told them? Why? When did you tell them? You told Michael and Charlotte?"

"Yes, I did."

"When?"

"When we moved in here."

"They've known all this time? Why?"

"I wanted them to know what kind of mother they have."

To Be Alone

Seventy-five thousand people lived on West Eighty-Sixth Street. I could make meals and deliver them. I'd have a set menu, and it would be like a club. You'd join for the month, and you'd get dinner for two every night. Basic menu. I could make soups or casseroles. I could make chocolate chip cookies with macadamia nuts. Pound cake or the cranberries my mother used to make. Later on, when the business picked up, I could rent out space, maybe even in the building, on the ground floor, and if it were a large enough space, I could even have it like a cafeteria. I would use china plates, I could get them cheap down in the Bowery. I'd use white napkins to cover the plates. No, not napkins, they'd soak up the food juices and look dirty. I'd put a plate over the plate, and I'd put everything in a basket and deliver it right to their doors, like they used to deliver milk. I could do it easily.

————

Elena told me Nadeshda Nikolaiovna, whom she knew from St. Petersburg and who now lived in Queens, was a great cook. I called Nadeshda Nikolaiovna, and she told me to come right over, she would give me whatever help I needed. I took the E train and walked to Metropolitan Avenue. She greeted me at her door. She was a short woman with thick, wavy gray hair. Her purple robe couldn't quite cover her pale pink nightgown. I could see the three rooms of her apartment from the hallway. Thick cotton curtains, in bright geometric patterns, were hung instead of doors.

"Amine, maybe you can help me? A man is coming here, he should have been here, he is not dependable. He started working, and he left and didn't come back. I'll show you."

I followed her into her bedroom. It smelled of iodine and lemons. The radio, on her nightstand, was turned to the Russian station, and a pleasant female voice was giving out the news. Nadeshda Nikolaiovna pointed to a newly plastered wall opposite her bed. The buzzer sounded.

"There he is now." She went to open the door. She came back, a tall, thin man wearing a wool hat behind her.

"Amine, can you please translate for me? Tell him to please finish his work. That if he starts, he cannot leave. He worked one hour."

"Can you tell her I couldn't get back into her apartment? Why doesn't she give me her key?" He spoke with an accent I couldn't place.

"I cannot give him my key. I will not. I do not trust him. I want to be here when he is here."

"She says she would feel better if she were here with you."

He promised to begin and finish the same day. He wanted all the things out of her room; otherwise he would have to do it, and this would delay him unnecessarily.

"You can see she is an elderly woman and sick. How can you ask her to move anything?"

"Let her go to a nursing home."

"Shame on you," I hissed at him when Nadeshda Nikolaiovna went to turn off the radio.

"I will bring the paint tomorrow, but tell her it is white. Now I have to paint the whole room."

"Oh please, I want pink. It is hard for me to be in a room with no color."

"The landlord wants everything painted white. He is sick of everything painted a different color. Everything has to be white."

"The landlord doesn't live here. She wants it pink. For god's sake, what's it to you if you paint it pink?"

"I cannot get pink paint. Only white paint is given to me."

"You can get a little can of red paint and put a little of the red paint into the white paint."

"Where am I going to get a little can of red paint?"

"At any paint store."

"Where is there a paint store? There is no paint store around here. The landlord wants white paint. That is what I do. Okay?"

She holds up her hands, "Okay, okay. I will look to the white walls and wish every day and every night they were pink." She left the room. I gave him twenty dollars and told him to do it. He left, and I went into the living room.

It had rained the night before and again that morning. The sun was out, and fresh air came in through the open window. She motioned for me to sit at the large table piled with books and papers. She sat in the chair next to me.

"Let God take care of him. Elena tells me you want to cook for money. I will give you all the help I can. I make a borscht that is not unliked. A friend's husband sat once and ate five bowls and for breakfast asked for more. I take turkey wings, maybe you can use a nice piece of chuck. It has to be lean. Only get it at a butcher store. I don't use it, it's too expensive for me. How many beets depends on how big a pot you have. I would say six, eight beets. Cook them until a fork goes through them. I like to add white kidney beans, they add a little thickness. Oh, when you are cooking the beets, squeeze a lemon, it will make the borscht stay red. Two large onions, chopped, and then you shred carrots. Three, four carrots and a green cabbage. Remember, these take very little time, so put them in toward the end. Squeeze another three, four lemons, salt, pepper, and always a little sugar. It should be like wine. How about some tea? My memory is always better when I am drinking tea. You sit. I have a rule, when I am visiting someone, I sit, and when someone is visiting me, they sit, and I get up."

I followed her to her kitchen, where she prepared tea the way my mother did. I carried the teapot, two cups and saucers, a small glass pitcher of milk, and a small flowered china bowl filled with cherry preserves, on a tray, to the table. She brought in a freshly baked cake.

"I made it a few days ago. It is still good. You will like it. You can be a very good cook but not a good baker. Baking needs a light hand. I never let anyone sit in the kitchen. The window looks out to the brick wall. I've been cooking a long time. I am seventy-four years old. I say it, and yet I cannot believe what I am saying. I go three times a week for dialysis. I spend my whole day there. It is hard, but what can you do? I always thought if, God forbid, I would get sick, I'd do away with myself. But no, you have a need to live. I was married. My first husband, I have a picture of him, I will show it to you. He saved my life from starvation. We were in Leningrad during the blockade. He was with the army, on the outskirts of the city. He would come and bring me his ration of bread, and he would eat sand. What reminded me were the walnuts in this cake. I grind them as fine as I can, but still . . . what people remember. Forty-two babies were born on the day my son was born. We mothers lay in the hospital. As the bombs dropped, the beds rolled to the center of the room. Only two were born alive. The mothers did not have the fluid to keep their babies. My son was the one who stayed alive; the other baby died the day it was born. They piled them in the corner like logs. When I was seven months pregnant, they came to get me to work, digging holes for the German tanks to fall through. My husband was there when they came. They pulled me by one arm, and my husband pulled me by my other arm. Finally they let me go when my husband told them he would give them three potatoes. They and the ones who they pulled in to work were blown up by a bomb that lay on the path of the trolley that was taking them to dig the holes for the tanks. My husband found me in bed with the man who became my second husband. This was after the war; my husband was still with the army. He would go away for long periods of time. He found us. Maxim covered himself with a sheet. I told him not to worry, and I calmly got up to speak with my husband. Before I said anything, he said, 'I have not seen anything, I have not heard anything, I do not know anything. I will give up all of mine, and you will give up all of yours, and we will live together nicely and in happiness.' I said no. That I had already put up for a divorce, on November sixteenth, and so had Maxim. That was how it was. That is Maxim's portrait over there. I was sitting next to him when that photograph was taken. I was holding a bouquet of flowers. I thought I looked bad, and I took a pair of scissors one day and cut myself out. How stupid that I did that. He is looking down at me. I lived with him for twenty-six years. We lived in love and happiness. Wherever we went, people thought we were lovers instead of husband and wife. I was never beautiful, but men were always drawn to me. Now you see me. I am alone, and there is no one. I often think that it all happened to someone else. I think that it is better to have a harder life earlier than later. Your youth carries you through. When you are old and alone, then you are really alone. My son, when I die, he will too. There is no one to take care of him. He has . . . MS. There's a woman, Tonia, she takes care of him, but she's going back to St. Petersburg. I pay a man ten dollars for coming, once a week, to wash him. Emma, his wife, refuses to pay. She says to me, 'The government gives you five hundred and forty dollars a month. The rent on your apartment is minimal. You can give your son some comfort.' Leeza has a good job. She is a programmer. She has insurance. She says the company is cutting back, and if she starts claiming for his needs, they will cut her off. Leeza is not a bad person, but she is very nervous and not pleasant to be around. My son and she have been together for thirty years. Their son, I have a picture of him and his wife, I will show it to you later, they bought a house in Connecticut. He is twenty-nine, his wife is twenty-seven. Do you know what my grandson said to me? 'If I were him, I would hang myself.' After he said this, I could not look into his eyes. And that, my dear, is how it is to be alone. Make your husband a wonderful dinner, set the table with clean white linen, light candles. Kiss him when he leaves, and kiss him when he comes back. It is awful to be alone. It was a fairy tale with my first husband. He saved my life. A friend of mine said you have to take two buckets of blood from a man. You give him nothing, you take from him. A woman needs love. It is her life. I had many lovers, but my son never knew. He knew I had admirers, but he did not know I slept with them. Georgian men are the most magnificent when they are courting you. But once they have had you, it's nothing. But while they court you, it is paradise. Men always were attracted to me. Married, unmarried, they all came."

A few days later I sold the Rolex Phillip had had Charlotte give me for my birthday. I got a thousand dollars for it.

Christmas Eve

We always trimmed the tree on Christmas Eve. The children went through the boxes of ornaments, untangling the lights, the little ones that twinkle on and off. It was seven o'clock, and I was in the kitchen making dinner. With each laugh I heard, I wanted to break a dish, throw myself out the fourteenth-floor window, or disappear. I always make a roast for Christmas Eve, a vegetable, and a salad. I could do it blindfolded. I put the roast and potatoes in the oven. The broccoli and carrots were cut up, waiting to be steamed, the salad with its ten ingredients was in the refrigerator, and the salad dressing was made. The horseradish would be grated at the last minute. I untied my apron, laid it down on the butcher block, and went into the living room. The children were on the oriental, arranging the ornaments by color. Phillip was on the couch, reading the *Post*, his glass of wine on the floor. Molly lay under the grand piano. Bing Crosby was singing "White Christmas." The fire was burning in the fireplace. I stood in the archway between the living and dining room. No one saw me.

"Would anyone like to go with me to St. John's Cathedral for midnight mass?" Silence.

"Come on, Stephen. Come with me."

"No, Mom, I don't want to."

"Come on. Let's all go after dinner. It'll be nice."

"It's freezing rain outside, Mom," Katherine said.

"So? We'll take umbrellas, and we'll bundle up. Let's go. Please."

"Did you hear her?" Phillip said, without looking up from the paper. "It's freezing outside."

"So?"

"Stop making them do something they don't want to do."

"Making them? All I'm asking is for someone to go with me."

"Why don't you save your hysterics?"

"Phillip, can I talk to you in the other room? Please."

I walked out to the hall and into Charlotte and Katherine's room. Phillip followed me and shut the door behind him.

"I can't stand it anymore. I've got to go."

"Leave."

"Why can't you do something?"

"Like what?"

"Say something to me."

"Amine, you are psychotic."

"I'm going to get my coat on, and I'm going to leave."

"Go ahead."

"What about dinner?"

"We can fix it ourselves. It's not really that hard, is it?" He left the room.

I forced myself to walk to the hall closet, put on a sweater and a coat, doubled a scarf around my neck, and pulled on a pair of warm weatherproof boots. The door behind me closed. Mercifully, the elevator didn't stop at any other floor going down.

Carlos saw me walk under the high stone arch, and he came out of his booth.

"Mrs. Calt, I would like to thank you and your family for your gift to me and my family."

"Carlos, forgive me."

"Forgive you? For what?"

Phillip had given each doorman a ten-dollar check for Christmas. When I told him I'd feel ashamed, he said, "You? Ashamed?"

The Upper West Side gets cold when the wind blows off the Hudson. I tied the scarf around my head and walked toward Riverside Drive. There was a man with his collie. At Seventy-Ninth Street I turned toward Broadway. Zabar's was closed. I walked past Barnes and Noble. The scarf couldn't keep the freezing rain away. I stood at a curb and saw Michael and Stephen on the other side of the street.

I waited for them to cross.

"Michael."

"We're getting some Christmas lights. The ones we have don't work."

"Michael." I grabbed the sleeve of his jacket and pulled him under an overhang. Stephen followed and hid his face in the back of my wet coat.

"You listen to me, and you listen good. If you don't make the woman you're with feel loved, she is going to leave your bed, and she will never come back. Do you hear me?"

"Don't talk like that in front of Stephen. We have to go."

From a pay phone I called Diana. She told me to come over. Instead, I walked to the George Washington Bridge and waited in the bus terminal for the next bus to Nyack. I let it pass when it came, and I took the subway back to Eighty-Sixth Street. Everyone was asleep. The tree was trimmed with no lights. The kitchen was cleaned up. The roast was hardly touched.

Cash

Phillip said he could no longer afford the apartment. There were three years left on the lease, and the contract said it could be sublet. We were moving back to Sheppard Road.

In January the apartment was rented to an advertising executive, his wife, and their two children. They were expecting a baby in March.

I told Phillip the apartment would have to be professionally cleaned.

"How much will that be?"

"Three hundred and twenty dollars plus a forty-dollar tip."

"You're kidding."

"They said to thoroughly clean this apartment will take two people eight hours. Twenty dollars an hour is three hundred and twenty dollars."

"Who gets twenty dollars an hour to clean?"

"They want to be paid in cash."

I took Phillip's money and cleaned the apartment myself. I was in the master bath, getting the area behind the toilet, when the phone rang.

"Madame Calt?"

"Yes."

"May I speak to you in Russian?"

"Yes."

"I am Vladimir's wife. Mila."

I took the lid off the jar that still stood on the small wood table between the two sinks and started rubbing the cream into my hands.

"Madame Calt?"

"I'm here."

"Forgive me for calling you, but I didn't know what else to do. Please help me. I listened to Vladimir's messages on his machine, and I heard your voice. You have such a soft voice, and you spoke so kindly. You are not like the others. They would demand to know where he was. Their tones were hard, unpleasant. I felt that you are a kind person and that I could talk to you. May I talk to you?"

"Yes."

"May I call you Amine?"

"Yes."

"Amine, you know about me?"

"Yes."

"He told you?"

"Yes."

"What did he tell you?"

"He told me he had been with you but that he no longer is."

"Vladimir and I are married, and we live together as husband and wife."

"I'm sorry, I didn't know."

"Yes. We were never officially married, but we have been together as husband and wife for eighteen years."

"I'm sorry."

"We were students together in Moscow."

"You have children?"

"A daughter."

"How old is she?"

"Twenty."

"She's not his daughter?"

"No, but he raised her."

"Does your daughter like him?"

"No. Amine, listen, I need your help. He's in Europe right now
with a young woman. He wants to marry her. She is going to in-
herit thirty million dollars very soon. He is with her only for the
money. He calls me every night from Europe and tells me he loves
me. He doesn't know that I know he is with her."

"How do you know?"

"Her lover told me."

"She has a lover?"

"She did. Jim is his name. She told Jim she was in love with
Vladimir. Jim has tried to warn her about Vladimir, but she will not
listen. She thinks Jim is jealous. He came to me, Jim, to see if I
could do anything."

"How did he know about you?"

"He had an investigation done on Vladimir, and then, of
course, he found out that Vladimir is with me."

"Where do you and Vladimir live?"

"In Riverdale. His office is in Manhattan. I would say to him,
'Stay the night in your office. You have a sofa that unfolds, sleep
there. Why come home when you are so tired?' Of course he
stayed. He stayed many nights, and he was never alone. He was
their doctor."

"Whose doctor?"

"The young woman's. Her name is Ester. They came to
Vladimir because Jim couldn't walk and they heard about Vladimir

and they thought Vladimir could help them. Vladimir made Jim walk again, and then Ester started seeing Vladimir because her skin was very bad, and of course Vladimir made it go away. Vladimir is very powerful, very gifted. Of course, she fell in love with him. He doesn't love her, he only wants her money. You never gave him any money?"

"No."

"Good. He wants to marry this girl. Please help me. They are coming back in a few days. Please talk to her, tell her you were with him. Tell her he likes being with other women."

"Would that help?"

"Of course."

"What would it do?"

"She would leave him, knowing he is the type of man who goes with other women, and then she will realize he is only after her money."

"Why did you stay with him?"

"I love him. I don't want her to have him. I know she does things with him that I will not do."

"Mila, maybe this is a chance for you to start a new life."

"It's too late for me. I left him once when I met someone else— he wanted to marry me. Vladimir pulled me back; he started phoning me and telling me he loved me. I went back to him."

"Leave him again."

"I can't. Amine, I am too old. It's too late for me. Before maybe, but not now. I missed my chance. I am going to be left standing alone by a broken gate. I have to have him back. It's my only chance. I know he loves me. Why would he say he does if he doesn't? Amine, I beg of you, will you help me?"

I asked her for her phone number and told her I would call back.

A week later Mila called. She told me I didn't have to call the young woman. She had gone over to Ester's apartment and told her Vladimir had made love to her when he returned from Europe. She wanted Ester to know. She mentioned he had affairs with several other women including me. When she was there, the phone rang, and Ester told Mila to answer it.

Mila told me he didn't recognize her voice when she said hello.

He said, "Darling, where are you?"

And only after Mila replied that she was held up in traffic, did he realize it was her on the other end.

He told Mila he never wanted to see her again and hung up.

Ester threw everything Vladimir had given her and the clothes he kept at her apartment out into the hall. Vladimir went back to Mila.

The couple renting the New Hampshire townhouse wanted to buy it. They also wanted to buy the furniture. I told Phillip I wanted the furniture for Sheppard Road—it would help fill up the empty house. The Harvey Brothers took the piano out the same way they had brought it in.

Extravagance

A friend of the family that was subletting the apartment came in through the open front door to drop off a housewarming gift, a food basket from Zabar's, as I was taking out the last load from the dryer. The friend finished her walk through the empty rooms and left. I found an opening in the cellophane wrapped around the Zabar basket, took out the brie and a box of stoned wheat crackers, and had lunch on the kitchen floor in the sunlight.

We left the antique mirror in the master bath, the custom-made shutters for the sixteen windows, and three copper frying pans, of varying sizes, in the oven drawer that wouldn't open.

Phillip and Michael waited at the house for the Harvey Brothers truck to arrive from New York City. Charlotte was swimming.

I picked Stephen up from a birthday party at Chelsea Piers, and we drove to Westchester.

Phillip told me not to go into his room. I told him not to go up to the attic.

The attic was where I wanted to be when we moved back to Sheppard Road.

He said he'd make his own dinner and do the grocery shopping.

I told him I wasn't cleaning his bedroom or bathroom. He told me he already told me not to go into his room.

"I'm not doing your laundry."

"I don't want you doing it."

"You have to give me some money every week."

"Why don't you rip out the gold faucets you had to have and sell them?"

Katherine was majoring in history and made All American. Michael graduated and was living at home. He found a job selling windows that did not let heat in or out, and aluminum siding. Charlotte and Stephen continued going to their schools in Manhattan. Charlotte drove Stephen in every day. After dropping Stephen off in the afternoon, she'd grab something to drink and drive to swim practice. I told Stephen to invite his friends to the house and I would drive them back to the city. He wouldn't, and when I asked him why, Charlotte said, "Mom, don't you get it?"

"What?"

"It's embarrassing for him."

"Why?"

"You're living in the attic."

"So?"

"Don't talk to me."

She wouldn't come up to the attic. She'd call me on the second line if she wanted anything. I stayed in the attic and read.

There was no birdseed left for Lorritta and Vanya, and I went to the pet shop. Ted had moved to Tucson for his asthma.

Gerald, the new owner, was leaning back in his swivel chair with his feet up on a stack of canned dog food when I walked in.

"Are you back? The city's not what you'd thought it'd be. Right?"

I smiled and made my way to the bin where the birdseed is kept. He came over, and we each filled a plastic bag.

"You've lost weight."

"Actually, I gained a little. I really lost it when my wife left. She found herself a guy up in Rhinebeck at a retreat that she and her girlfriends went to. Meditation and all that crap. Jesus, something happens to them, they sort of go nuts."

"Was your wife going through menopause?"

"Yeah, that's right, she was. How did you know?" He laughed. "Right. You would. This guy of hers up and died on her. Maybe he bent down one too many times. She's paying for it now though. Big time. She's taking care of her sick mother. Do you still have dogs?"

"Just Molly."

"What happened to the other one?"

"I had to put him down."

"Yeah, you gotta do that sometimes. It's tough."

We walked over to the cash register, and I took a wrapped piece of candy from a glass jar that stood on top of one of the hamster cages.

"She tried divorcing me, but it was lame and the judge threw it out."

"You don't want to give your wife a divorce?"

"What? Are you kidding? She's not getting half of anything. She's really gotten old looking; she never took anything for it. How's your husband? I remember he played the piano. Right? I told my wife we'd be going to one of his concerts someday. Say hello to him for me."

He followed me out to the car carrying two twenty-five-pound bags of dried dog food. He put them on the front seat while Molly barked at him from the back.

"Give your parrots broccoli; it's full of calcium. That way they'll live forever. Nice seeing you again. Take care of yourself."

That night I told Phillip I wanted a separation agreement.

"We don't have any money to divide up. You saw to that. The move to New York cost three hundred thousand."

"I have to get a lawyer."

"You're dreaming, Amine. I'm telling you again, there's nothing. There's nothing to divide."

"I need money."

"You don't get it, do you?"

Annette Kramer was in her fifties, married thirty years with three sons.

Her office looked out on the Westchester County Courthouse. The bookcase lining the wall behind her desk had framed photographs of Annette smiling next to famous people. She wore a short black skirt, and her stiletto heels lay on the carpet by the coat rack.

I had trouble answering her questions regarding our finances.

"I know we had to refinance everything because of the renovation, and we had to sell Florida and New Hampshire because of it. The renovation. I know the house we live in has a big mortgage on it, and the house on Nantucket is mortgaged, and the adjacent property on Nantucket has a mortgage on it. I don't know what the mortgages are. He said I demanded the best and that I'm extravagant."

"What you did, Mrs. Calt, was add value and enhance your properties. That is not extravagant. This is extravagant." She put her hands in front of her face and wriggled eight fingers. On them were diamond, ruby, and sapphire rings. She told me she would need a twenty-five-hundred-dollar retainer. I told her I didn't have it. She said, "Sorry."

That night I told Phillip I had to start seeing a therapist and he had to pay for it. I began seeing Alan, who Diana recommended again, once a week. We talked about my father and mother. He suggested I take Prozac for a while. I told him I didn't even take aspirin. He suggested I come to him twice a week if I could. I did, and Phillip paid for it.

Charlotte's friend's mother, Louise, called me. She and I had been in the volunteer ambulance corps together years ago. She told me Charlotte talked to her about our family situation, and unfortunately she could relate to it—she was breaking up with her husband, whom she had been married to for thirty years. She asked me if I remembered Sidney Greene. I said, of course. He lived down the road from us, and he was still active in the ambulance corps and the fire department. Louise told me he was her lawyer, and she had spoken to him about me.

"Louise, I don't have money for a retainer."

"I know. I don't think he'll take it. Why don't you call him?"

The next Saturday I walked to Sidney and Joyce's house, and he and I sat outside on the terrace while Joyce put in tulip bulbs, replacing what was eaten by the deer.

I told Sidney I had had an affair and Phillip found out about it. Sidney told me I could fuck a different guy in Macy's window for a week and it didn't matter. The courts were only interested in the welfare of the children and who got what, and after listening to me, there didn't seem to be much. The only property he thought I might get some money from was the adjoining two-acre building lot on Nantucket that Phillip and I had bought years ago to protect our views and that was now on the market. Sidney would see to it that I got at least fifty thousand when we sold it. "Fifty thousand ain't peanuts, and it'll get you through for a while. I'd be happy to sit down with the two of you and maybe get to some conclusions."

When I got back to the house, I found Phillip in the basement sorting out athletic equipment we were donating to the middle school. I told him about Sidney and how he said he'd be happy to sit down with the two of us. Phillip said he wasn't sitting down with anyone.

Sidney sent Phillip a letter stating I had retained him. He "hoped the matter could be resolved as unemotionally and inexpensively as possible," and Phillip was to "retain counsel so that a meaningful dialogue toward an amicable solution could be started."

Phillip replied that he and I were very behind with many of our financial obligations, including taxes and tuition payments, and we weren't in any position to engage matrimonial lawyers. That the matter would be best addressed by therapy, which he had been providing for and would continue to provide for. He thanked Sidney for his concern.

Sidney replied that unfortunately for Phillip, marriage was not a unilateral situation, where one person decided for both husband and wife. Phillip would be forced to retain counsel by being served with a summons and complaint in the Supreme Court, Westchester County.

Phillip retained Nancy Parker, Esq.

German Sauna

Rosa called and said my father had had a heart attack but was now home. I told her I had to go to Nantucket and that maybe, if I could, when I got back in the fall, I'd come over. She said yes, of course, that that would be fine. I drove to Nyack the next day. I hadn't seen them in twelve years. I'd crossed the Tappan Zee Bridge when I remembered I'd left the photographs of the children on a platter in the kitchen. I went back to get them.

They were sitting on the porch in the wicker settee when I pulled up. They walked down the steps holding hands as I got out of the car. Rosa had stopped dying her hair black, and my father had become an old man.

Rosa made *pelmeni,* small meat-filled dumplings cooked in chicken broth and served with sour cream and fresh chopped dill. When we used to make them together, she would tell me about Harbin before the Japanese occupation and how she had hidden when her first husband got drunk. She fled Mao and became a refugee in Istanbul, where she married an American GI. I told my mother, once, she should try putting a little water in the raw meat for the *pelmeni*; it made them juicier. My mother replied that it also made them tasteless. That you never put water in meat, unless you're making a soup, and that if I tried telling her again what that bitch said or did, I'd get what for.

Rosa asked about the children, and I took the pictures out of my bag. She kept shaking her head as she looked at them, telling me how they had grown. She handed the pictures to my father, and he put them on the coffee table without looking at them.

Rosa asked about Phillip, and I told her we were separating. She said how could that be; she never saw two people more in love. My father said in a hoarse whisper that Phillip was never one of us. Rosa told him not to say that. Phillip loved his family, and for that he should be respected.

We sat at the table. My father told Rosa he wasn't hungry and pushed his bowl away. He sat staring at the white lace tablecloth, cleared his throat, and started the stories I had heard many times. His mother died when he was three. He was four and his sister was five when she told him to put his finger in the cabbage grinder. She turned the handle, and he lost the first joint of his pinkie. She didn't do it right, his stepmother said—instead of his finger, it should have been his tongue. He was thrown down into the base-ment with the rats when he misbehaved. At ten, after his step-mother told him to leave, he traveled thousands of miles by train to find his uncle. He was seventeen during the famine and left for Leningrad when he found out his aunt was giving him food while she went hungry. He graduated from the military academy and was a lieutenant in the Finnish War. He watched artillery shells break the ice in front and in back of a battalion of Soviet soldiers. They didn't know they were on a frozen lake, and they sank into the water like lead pipes. He was a captain when he was captured by the Germans two days after Stalin declared war and spent three years in a prisoner of war camp.

My father gripped the arms of his chair and got up. The prisoners called it the German sauna. Winter. Rows of men, twelve abreast, naked except for those wooden clogs. The order was given to run. And they ran between two lines of German soldiers spraying them with cold water. And then the order was given to stand, and we stood. Thousands died.

Rosa told my father to sit down, it wasn't good for him to remember, and he told her he wanted me to know. I had always thought of my father as a weak man, who needed to be protected. He didn't ask about the children, and he didn't look at the photographs Rosa had brought to the table.

He walked out of the room, and I heard him climb the uncarpeted stairs. I moved to clear the table. Rosa told me to sit and went into the kitchen carrying the dishes on a big silver tray. I put the photographs back in my bag. My father came back with a carton of eight-millimeter movies he had taken of me at Bear Mountain when I was sixteen and of Natalie and me at Palisades Amusement Park, Jones Beach, the Catskills, Reis Park. I said I should go, they were predicting high winds and a thunderstorm, and sometimes the Tappan Zee Bridge was closed.

My father wouldn't let me carry the carton to the car. I opened the trunk, and he put the carton in. I stood still as he reached to hold me. He asked why and how did it all happen and what was it that he did? His eyes filled with tears, and I didn't comfort him. Rosa came out with an umbrella, and they stood under it as I backed out of the driveway.

Simple

Phillip said we had to have some papers notarized in order to sell the land on Nantucket, and did I know of a notary in town? A couple had signed a contract on the property, but they would only buy the land if the town allowed them to build a large house on it.

As we drove down the hill I told Phillip my lawyer thought I should get fifty thousand dollars when we sold it. Phillip said we had to pay off our debts first and if there was anything left.

I stood at the counter of the county clerk's office and signed the documents.

Carole called, "Where have you been?"

"At the library. Why didn't you leave a message?"

"I hate those machines. Why don't you get yourself a job instead of wasting your time at the library? What's new?"

"Nothing. Everything's the same. I'm downstairs when he's at work, I'm upstairs when he comes home. Actually he came home early yesterday. We had to go downtown to sign some papers. He was actually nice, and we talked."

"You signed papers?"

"Um."

"What did you sign?"

"I forget what he said they were. They were just papers."

"Does Sidney know?"

"No. Why? What's so unusual about my signing some papers?"

"Amine, are you getting a divorce, or is this some nightmare you're having? Why are you signing papers without your lawyer knowing about it?"

"Carole, I have always signed papers Phillip told me to sign. I don't understand why you're making such a big deal out of it."

"You know, you're dangerous. Call Sidney right now."

I didn't call Sidney, I called Phillip. He told me I signed a paper saying I was a U.S. citizen, because I was born in Germany, another paper that said there was no formaldehyde on the property, another that there was no lien on it and the deed. I asked Phillip if that was it. He said yes.

I told Carole everything was fine. We were waiting for the land to sell, and as soon as it did, I'd be able to get an apartment in the city for myself and Stephen. I'd rent for a while until we got our finances straightened out, and then maybe I'd buy something. Something small, a two-bedroom near Columbia University, looking out to the river, a lot of sun, the windows would look west. When the children came, I'd have these new air mattresses that instantly blow up. I'd figure it out. I didn't care if Phillip had anything hidden. I knew there was Sheppard Road and Nantucket and the land that we were selling and his pension, and I knew I'd get half of everything. Phillip could have everything else. I wanted it to be over.

Phillip got Michael an interview with Bear Stearns. The first question they asked was if he had any sales experience. He told them he tried selling windows and aluminum siding. They hired him. He continued to live at home until he saved enough money to move into the city. Stephen was busy with school and friends. He wanted to start playing football. Phillip thought Stephen should wait until he grew some more. Katherine again made All American. Charlotte was majoring in psychology at Purdue, and she was excited to be swimming for a Big Ten school.

My father died. Rosa said he sat up in bed and looked toward the door, and it was as if he saw someone there because he smiled. Natalie flew in from Nantucket for the funeral. I told Phillip I wanted Stephen to come with me. He told me he didn't want his son going to the funeral of such an awful man, and if I dared take Stephen out, he'd get a court order to prevent me. I told him to go ahead.

There were more than a hundred people at my father's burial. People I hadn't seen in years came up to tell me what a wonderful man my father was. How intelligent, how funny, how generous, and how kind. How proud I must be to have had a father like him.

On the way back to Sheppard Road, Natalie told me she was on Main Street and someone told her our land had sold. I told her it hadn't, that a couple was interested in it.

I called the real estate office when we got home, and Johanna told me the closing on the land had been done that afternoon.

I called Sidney.

"Amine, this better be important. I'm on vacation."

"We sold the Nantucket property."

"Congratulations."

"Sidney, I didn't know it sold. There was a closing on it."

"It closed?"

"Yes. Today. I just happened to call the real estate agent because my sister heard it from someone on Main Street that it sold. I didn't believe—"

"Are you home?"

"Yes."

"Stay there. I'm calling Nancy. I'll call you right back."

An hour later Sidney called.

"You made me out to be an asshole. I'm giving Nancy the riot act, and she tells me you signed the deed. You lied to me. Get yourself another lawyer. I'm not working for you anymore. I will not have a client lie to me."

"Sidney, I didn't lie to you."

"You told me you knew nothing about the sale of the property."

"I didn't."

"You signed the fucking deed."

"Does signing a deed mean you sold the property?"

"Listen to me. Are you listening to me, Amine? When you sign a deed, that's it."

"What do you mean that's it?"

"Amine, do you have a lawyer? Yes or no, answer me. Goddamn it. Do you or do you not have a lawyer?"

"Yes."

"When you have a lawyer, you sign nothing, fucking nothing, without his knowledge and approval. I do not want you as a client anymore. No way. I'm out. I'm not putting up with this shit. Get yourself another asshole."

"Sidney, I'm sorry, you know I can't get another lawyer. I don't have any money. Please, Sidney."

"Didn't I tell you, when you walked over and you and I sat out that afternoon, that you don't have anything except for the property on Nantucket? That you don't have any equity in your houses? Didn't I? Yes or no?"

"Yes."

"And didn't I also tell you I would get you at least fifty thousand from the sale of that property? Yes or no?"

"Yes."

"Amine, kiss the money good-bye because you ain't gettin' it. You dumb schmuck. You signed it away. I cannot believe this. Let me get off the phone before I find a way of killing you from St. Bart's."

"Sidney, I'm sorry."

"You're sorry? Let me get off the phone. My wife's screaming at me for yelling at you. What a piece of work you are, Amine."

"Sidney, how can he get the money? Whatever check was made out by the buyers had to be made out to the both of us. Right? The property is in both our names."

"Amine, are dolphins swimming through this phone line and you can't hear me? Kiss the money good-bye. I've got to go take a swim. Sayonara."

The money was wire-transferred to a joint checking account I hadn't used in years and thought was closed. It went in, and the next day the money went out and into an account that had only Phillip's name on it.

I didn't sleep that night and went into Phillip's bedroom at five in the morning. He was in his bathroom, shaving. He told me I was the liar.

I made a fist and hit him on his back and then picked up the aerosol shaving can and sprayed him and everything around him. I don't know if I propelled myself out of the room or if it was Phillip. I went up to the attic.

Michael and Natalie came up after Phillip left. I couldn't stop shaking. Michael put his arms around me. I told him my father died and maybe I had been watching too much of Jerry Springer. We laughed, and then I started to cry.

Sidney called and said Nancy Parker wanted to have a restraining order issued against me. Nothing like that was to happen again, or I would be out of the house, and he wouldn't be able to do anything about it. I told him I had to get out. I'd rent an apartment in town, I didn't care. I couldn't take it anymore. Sidney told me to get to his office, he didn't want to talk on the phone.

"Amine, Phillip is not going to let you have Stephen. He says you're unfit and unstable, and he's going to get the kids to testify to that."

"He'd never do that."

"He's doing it. And you know why he's doing it? He doesn't want to pay you. If Stephen lives with you, he has to pay seventeen percent of his gross earnings to you. And he wants to do that like he wants to live in the Holland Tunnel. I thought I could work it out for you, but he's shown his cards with the property. You are staying in your house with your son. It is your house, and you will be with your son because your son needs you. Do you hear me? If you do anything to jeopardize that, like this last incident, I will personally beat the crap out of you. Do you understand? Did you hit him hard?"

"Sidney, I can't stand it."

"Neither can he. It's just become a waiting game. Will the children testify?"

"I'll never allow it to get to that. Who would do that?"

"The guy who wants to win."

"I don't want to win."

"I do."

"Please, Sidney, I can't stay."

"You're staying."

I drove Natalie to Westchester Airport for her to get a flight back to Nantucket, and I asked her if she would testify for me in court.

"I don't know if I can do that. I think it's better if Phillip and you work this out between you. Please don't get me involved in this."

In the evening Michael came up to the attic and sat at the edge of my bed.

"Mom, I will never testify. They'll have to drag me into court."

"Michael, what do I do?"

"I don't know, Mom."

I knocked on Phillip's door the next night.

"Amine, I acted on the basis of advice of counsel. All the money went to pay our debt. I have an itemized list I can give you. You'll see there were taxes and tuition payments I had to pay."

"That's right, it did, didn't it. But what about the money it freed up? What about that? Can't you now do with that what you want? Phillip, all I ever wanted was fairness. I told you I wanted you to treat me fairly. Was this fair?"

"Wake up, will you? We have enormous debt that I am trying to clear up. What do you think I'm doing with the money? Where do you think it goes? Look around. Who do you think keeps all this going?"

"You know, Phillip, I don't care. I never thought you could do anything like this. But that is nothing compared to your not allowing me to have Stephen."

"That's right, you don't care. You even wrote, 'I don't care about Phillip or the children.'"

"I don't remember writing anything like that."

"You don't remember a lot of things. You want me to show it to you? You think I'm going to allow Stephen to go down the tubes with you? You'll destroy him just like you destroyed the rest of us."

The King Alfreds

Carole called in the morning. She asked if I'd go to the ballet at Lincoln Center. She finally has a subscription, and no one in her family will go with her. She'll pick me up in her car, but I will have to drive in. She can't stand the maniacs on the road.

I knew Carole wouldn't come into the house. She's avoided Phillip ever since George came over and asked Phillip not to move the stone wall that stands between our properties. George and Carole buried both their Irish setters by it. Phillip had pulled out the new survey that showed his property going beyond the wall into "land George shouldn't think is his anymore." George couldn't claim it, said Phillip, by using their two dogs as an excuse. And he had the stone wall moved. Now fifteen feet of grass and two dead dogs are on our side of the stone wall.

———————

I walked out of the house into a cold May evening. Spring was late that year, the dogwoods were just coming out. It would be a brilliant fall.

I waited for Carole to finish beating her car mat against the corner of the garage.

Carole hadn't lost her looks or the blond in her hair. We both worried about our calcium. I ate cottage cheese and sardines. She took Tums, three rolls a day. She didn't smoke or drink coffee or eat processed meat. She liked her champagne with a splash of raspberry vodka, and she was wearing the black cashmere coat we flipped a quarter for at last month's St. Anthony's Rummage Sale.

She straightened up after putting back the mat and said, "I still miss the King Alfreds."

Carole was remembering the daffodils. It took us a week of afternoons to plant them. We laid the bulbs in five tight rows along the path leading to Katherine and Charlotte's playhouse. The daffodils came up stronger every May for fifteen years. When the new well needed to be dug, an underground spring was disturbed, and it flooded the whole area where the daffodils grew.

I backed Carole's Suburban to the front. I couldn't stop myself from looking toward the house and seeing Phillip sitting in his chair by the windows.

The night before, as he and I stood a few feet apart by the stairs going to the attic, he said, "Amine. Don't you understand? You are irrelevant to me."

It took only a few minutes to leave our country lane and be on the parkway going south. Carole unfastened her seat belt and said, "I don't want to get wrinkled."

I glanced over to her as she began to play with her hair. She'd take a strand and begin twirling it around her finger, using the twisted end, like a paintbrush, to dot her lips. She looked out the side window. "My mother had rosebushes. I wanted to dig them up from her yard and plant them where our tennis court used to be, but that cheap, miserable bastard sold them. She had a bush of blue ones. Roses don't smell anymore. They've strained the smell right out."

"Roses take so much time. I've tried covering them, not covering them. It doesn't seem to matter," I replied.

"Her roses grew from May to . . . November? Yeah, there were roses on the table at Thanksgiving. Funny, I just remembered that."

"We always had a bowl of fruit on the table for Thanksgiving."

"She made the best pies. She'd have the kids pick the apples off the ground. She'd make six, seven pies. They'd be gone in two days. I asked her to give me the recipe. She'd say, 'Watch me.' I was never in the kitchen long enough to watch."

I thought of my own mother and all the questions left unanswered.

"I'd have her out to the house we had in Shelter Island. She wouldn't be there two days when she'd say, 'Take me to the fruit stand. I want to get those peaches to make your father a pie.' A pie! When I saw the bastard take the bedpost and beat her with it. He kept it unscrewed and ready."

"Did she ever fight him back?" I asked.

Carole laughed. "Are you still hoping I'll say yes? I walked in on them once. He had her right on the kitchen table. He was mean. Mean. I'd ask him for a nickel to buy a Good Humor. You know what he'd say? 'Go earn it.' I was five years old. The only thing he ever gave me was a radio for my graduation, and he bought it at the Salvation Army thrift store. And she had to die before him. He left everything, the house, the apartment buildings, everything to the archdiocese. He really thought it would get him to heaven. May his soul rot in hell."

"Vera Simmons died."

"I know. Finally," Carole said.

"They say she went down to sixty pounds. You could see her heart."

"That's not possible," Carole said.

"Yes. They say you could see it beating."

"Promise me, Amine. If I ever get that way, leave me off somewhere in the desert. Give me a sun reflector, and tell me to just keep walking, that you'll pick me up real soon. Vera held on too long. There's a point where you've got to say, okay, that's enough. Thank you. Good-bye."

When is enough, enough? Vera was president of the garden club. There were eleven of us. We'd pile into two station wagons and go planting around statues. Carole and I are the only ones left. Everyone else has moved away. Vera's husband was transferred to Keene, New Hampshire.

"I have to tell you the latest," Carole said. "I get a call from a dealer this morning. There's a show at the county center. He tells me he's got what my husband wants. George has been looking for a BB gun like the one he had when he was twelve. His mother made him sell it. He got four dollars for it. Now, this dealer, how many years later? Has one just like it. In its original box, tissue paper, the whole thing. But now, of course, it's five hundred dollars. Today is George's birthday. Funny, he gets his wish on his birthday. He buys the gun, brings it home. By now he's had a few. I'm in the library, polishing the porridge bowl where I keep the Gummi Bears, and I see him standing in the doorway, pointing the gun at me. He says, 'Let me just blow away that beaver. It's not doing me any good.' I tell him, 'Go ahead.' " And she laughed. "If only he knew where the beaver was last night, how wet and wild it was. I really cannot stand him. We did nothing for his birthday. I wanted to go to the Kittle House for brunch, but he was out buying a gun. None of the kids showed up. Their father's sixty-fifth birthday. Can you imagine? 'I'll blow it away. It's not doing me any good.' " And she laughed.

"One of these days he might just do it."

"George? You know what he said to me? 'If I'd killed you when we still lived in Scarsdale, I'd be out by now.' He's funny." She laughed. "Amine, what do I have? Maybe another five good years? As soon as we sell the house, I'm out. I'll get a house in Westport, on the water, close to town, where I can walk to everything. I can take the train to the city. I've had it with the driving."

"I thought you were going to Florida?"

"No. The whole state is one big air conditioner. I told you Milos is buying a house in Captiva. I'll make him open all the windows when I visit. It's so convenient having him so close by. I'm really going to miss him. He says I'm like a river."

I wondered why they call it the Saw Mill River Parkway. There had to have been a river here. Once. Large enough to have a saw mill on it. Where did it go?

"Milos is the same age as George. Incredible. George can't get it up anymore. It's the drinking. It's sad. George was so good. Once. Still, not like Milos. It's also the genes. George's father left before George was born, so God knows what he was like. Milos's father is ninety, and they have to restrain him in the nursing home."

I thought how lucky Carole was that her parents died quickly. It wasn't quick for my mother. But then she was with me, and I held her hand when she died.

"The only problem with Milos is he repeats himself. He forgets, and I don't want to tell him, 'Milos, I've heard this.' Listen, as long as he fucks me the way he does, I don't care. I put a smile on my face and say, 'Oh Milos, what an interesting story.' He's a great cook too. George remembers everything when he's sober, which is not a lot of the time, and he can't get it up. Milos remembers close to nothing and can go on for days. Wouldn't it be great if I could splice them together and throw away what's not working?"

"With Phillip it's a mystery."

"Well Amine, while you're trying to figure that one out, climb down those attic stairs of yours and join the world. Find yourself a man. All I have to do is put it out to one of Milos's brothers, and you're in."

"I don't want that."

"I know. You want love. I was in Barnes and Noble the other day. I was looking through some books, and I read something. It said, 'Love is something you don't have, and you give it to someone who doesn't want it.' "

"That's not true."

"Why are you holding on? Are you waiting for him to say, 'Amine, you're the best thing that's ever happened to me'? He's never going to say it. Get over it. He's incapable of it. Leave him."

"I am."

"Right. You'll be up in that attic of yours for a while yet. You've made it too comfortable for yourself up there. And you won't let go. You keep your mother's ashes by your bed, for god's sake. And where would you go?"

"I'm going to UC Berkeley."

"To do what?"

"I am going to get a degree in archaeology."

"Being with one dead man is not enough for you? You haven't said anything to me about this. When did you decide this?"

"Last night."

"Last night? You're not serious. You're not going to do this. Anyway, you're too old."

"I'm not. I'm doing it."

"It's too late to apply."

"I'm applying for the summer session. I'll be enrolled by fall."

"When are you leaving?"

"At the end of May."

"No, you're not."

"I am."

"You're leaving Stephen?"

"He'll come with me."

"You're joking."

Carole and I sat still, watching the New York City Ballet perform *Sleeping Beauty*. A bar of dark chocolate rested in my lap. I tried not to let the rustle of the thin foil be heard as I gave Carole and myself a piece. Carole leaned over and whispered, "Isn't it magical?"

By the Clock

A light October rain started to fall. On my way to the coat closet to get an umbrella, I saw part of the ceiling lying on the grand piano. I told Phillip there might be a leak in the shower. He said all we had to do was reposition the shower head so the water would fall into the drain and wouldn't collect along the sides where the leak probably was. I guessed the ceiling couldn't take it anymore. I cleaned the piano, moved it out of the way, and covered the floor with blankets that were still in the closet from the time the children used them to make teepees.

I was to meet Sidney in Grand Central by the clock. He and I would walk to Nancy Parker's office. It had been ten months since the four of us had a meeting. Nothing had changed. Phillip and I were still on Sheppard Road. It was now a question of who moved out.

I was taking the train into the city. I wouldn't have to deal with the traffic or the expense of midtown parking. I gave myself fifteen minutes to walk down the hill to the station.

I barely made the train.

I noticed the young man sitting diagonally across from me. I had seen him on the platform as I was catching my breath. He was so clean. He had on a new suit. Did he shave? He must. I wasn't near enough to know if he used cologne. Probably. He was still talking on his cellular phone.

"I'll figure it out. . . . You know what?" "The truth is." "Profit." "You know." "I'd buy it." "Sure." "Exactly." "No rush." "As long as it's in our possession." "I'll call you when I get to the office."

A thick gold band encircled his left ring finger. They probably bought one of those prefab modular homes starting at $790,000 on Hardscrabble Road. Did they choose to have it assembled on level ground or on a knoll? They probably wanted to get those fast-growing pines in before the ground froze. They'll have them planted along the edge of their acre to block the sight of the power lines.

I thought of Lillian Hellman. She lived on Hardscrabble Road, and the new development was part of her farm where she grew bleached asparagus and raised poodles. I was in her farmhouse once, now owned by friends of friends. I sat in the library where she wrote, and I was shown the linen closet where the shelves had been left labeled "Miss Hellman," "Mr. Hammett." She had sold the farm to pay for Dashiell Hammett's defense. For her there was no choice.

The young man sneezed. A balding man in a pin-striped, white-collared shirt said, "Bless you."

"Thanks."

He was coming down with a cold. He was overworked, and he went outside with his hair wet.

He stood up and walked to the doors as the train pulled into 125th Street. The doors opened, and he got off.

Of course. He was one of the ones who was going to make Harlem viable.

I pretended not to see Phillip in the building's lobby. We took separate elevators up. We were all right on time.

"The tuition for the Columbia University course Amine wants

to take is completely unaffordable. If she wants to further her education, then she should take classes at Westchester Community College," said Phillip's lawyer, looking smart in a size-two Calvin Klein, ticking off at three-fifty an hour, Elsa Peretti's gold misshapen heart dangling from her throat.

"We'll get to that. First, I'd like to discuss Amine and Phillip's living situation. Phillip should move to an apartment in the city. Amine and Stephen should live in the house while Stephen is still in school, which is for another five years. Then, if Phillip wants the house, he can buy Amine out."

"That's unacceptable. Amine hates the house. Has always hated the community. She's stated this time and again. Phillip loves the house. Let Amine be the one to rent an apartment in the city. She should live where she has always wanted to live. Phillip works in the city, and he loves coming home to the fresh air."

"Stephen is in school and Amine stays with her son until he graduates."

"Let her rent a house."

"Amine is not renting a house. If Amine moves, it will be into a house of her own. This is nonnegotiable."

"Amine is well aware there is no money for her own house."

"The Nantucket house can be sold."

"The Nantucket house is for Phillip's retirement."

"You know very well, Nancy, if this goes to court, there will be a division of property, and aren't we here trying to avoid court at all costs?"

I wondered if the rest of the ceiling fell down.

Red Silk Lining

"How much do you think a Harley costs?"

"Fully loaded, between twenty-three and twenty-four."

"Carole, I think Phillip bought one. I found a big Harley-Davidson bag in his closet. There was a helmet in it and gloves. They're black on the palms, which means he's been wearing them for a while. And a pair of lace-up boots. I found another pair of heavier ones, pull-ons, hidden under some linen napkins that he uses to polish his shoes. My napkins. But you know what really got me? A red bandanna. You know how the Hell's Angels would tie bandannas around their heads low, covering their foreheads, almost to their eyes? He bought one that's sewn into a permanent knot. It's like a hat, and it's lined in red silk. Carole, what do I do?"

"Take pictures."

The following week Phillip left the house early on a Saturday morning. The next afternoon as I walked to the end of the drive, he returned and parked his car behind mine. It had snowed the previous night, and I wasn't able to get the car to the house after picking Stephen up from a basketball game.

"Phillip, back up so I can leave. I'm going into the city to see someone."

"I need to throw some ice melt down."

"Don't bother. The snow's almost gone, it's been warm today. You won't have a problem getting it up."

"Leave me alone."

I stood and watched him throw handfuls of white pellets in front of my car and behind his. He bent low to the ground, his feet wide apart, and I noticed he had on new shoes.

The next morning I went into his closet, and in the pocket of the coat he wore the day before, I found a crumpled receipt. A hotel on Fifty-Third off of Fifth Avenue. Three hundred and ninety-five for the room, one hundred and ten for food. Brunch? Five hundred and five, not including tax and gratuities. In the inside pocket of a jacket of a charcoal-gray-striped suit, two stubs from *Phantom of the Opera*. Center orchestra, sixth row up. I crawled under his bed where he kept his private phone and dialed star sixty-nine, certain whoever she was must have called, concerned if he got home safely. A recorded voice gave me a ten-digit number. A live operator told me it was a Hoboken exchange.

"Carole, I want you to call this number."

She called me back a few minutes later. "Young voice, sounds a little like you actually. Must be young. I asked her if Milos was there. She told me I had the wrong number. He probably stores it in her garage."

That night there was no hot water for a bath. Phillip yelled up to the attic that there was something wrong with the tank and that a man was coming to fix it later.

In the morning the house was cold. Phillip and Michael went to work. I woke Stephen up for school and went to the kitchen to start his breakfast. On the banister, going down to the laundry room, was a notice from the oil company: "Could not locate a check please call in A.M." I called, and the dispatcher told me my husband was supposed to have left a check. Their man was on his way, but he would give us oil only if he got a check.

Taped to the inside wall of the boiler room was one of Phillip's business envelopes: a Citibank check, number 121, made out to the Restassured Oil Company for twelve hundred. I called the automated teller service and punched in the number of the new account and Phillip's Social Security number. The balance, as of that morning, was ten thousand and change. Five checks totaling seventeen hundred had cleared the day before.

Phillip called from work later that morning.

"Did the guy come?"

"Why aren't you paying the oil company on time?"

"I asked if the guy came?"

"Answer me first. Why are we waiting until there's no more oil in the tanks to pay what we owe? I am telling Sidney, and he is going to hire a forensic accountant who will go over everything. Now with computers it's hard to hide things."

"So what you're saying is we're headed for court."

"That's right."

"We're not headed for divorce court. We're going to be in bankruptcy court."

"Tell me, Phillip, is it possible to be in bankruptcy court when your assets total more than your liabilities?"

"Amine, you're delusional. I am no longer going to be a blank check for you, and you are not going to be able to continue spending the kind of money you have been accustomed to spending. Reality, Amine, is going to smack you right in the face."

"Maybe you should garage your motorcycle here to save money."

"I do."

"You do?"

"I do."

"Where?"

"It's there."

"I haven't seen it."

"Maybe you haven't looked."

I went out to the garage, and there it was, behind the Porsche, two blankets I had bought for Michael when he went away to school, covering it.

I took the blankets off. It was black and shining. I looked at the Porsche, which had been sitting on blocks for eighteen years. They say if the undercarriage is rusted, it's not worth restoring. The old license plates were still on it. We had kept it for Michael. We wanted to give it to him as his graduation present.

Four Dollars and Fifty-one Cents

Carole's son Daniel owns a coffee shop, and he asked me if I would work there on weekends when it got busy. Carole must have told him I needed the money.

The first customer I served was a woman I had known from the country club. The awkwardness passed as soon as I made her her double espresso skim latte with a squeeze of chocolate.

A perfumer-pianist-historian came in on Saturdays and wanted only me to make him his triple espresso, the rim of the cup rubbed with a lemon peel. He said he closes his eyes, and he's in Florence. "I defy you," he said, handing me a brown glass bottle with a stopper, "to distinguish this Chanel Number Five from the one you're wearing." I could, but I told him I couldn't.

One Sunday as the bells of Grace Church rang out, signaling the end of worship, a woman walked in. Her blond hair was pulled back into a French twist, and she wore a blue wool crepe suit; linen violets were pinned to the lapel of her short jacket, and by the neckline of her white silk blouse, a strand of pearls.

"May I have a cappuccino with skim milk and a black currant scone?"

"The pearls you're wearing are lovely."

"Thank you. They were my mother's. She told me to wear them close to my skin. That the salt from the skin reminds the pearls of their home, and that is what makes them shine."

"Where are you from in England?"

"A hamlet, not far from London. It's by the sea, and it is still the same. John is my brother."

"John? Is John the reverend?"

"Oh, sorry. Yes, he is. I somehow still believe everyone knows each other. You have lovely skin."

An older couple walked in. They warmly greeted the English-woman, and the three of them sat at a table by the window, and I could hear them laughing.

The next Sunday the Englishwoman came in with a man.

"May I please have a cappuccino and a scone? Darling, are you having anything?"

"No. Nothing."

She had on gold Cartier earrings with a matching necklace. Carole had the same set.

I handed her her cup, and she asked if I had made it with skim milk.

"I'm sorry, I didn't."

"That's fine. It really doesn't matter," she said.

"No. Let me remake it for you." I took the cup that she had placed on the counter. "You should have it the way you want it. You're paying for it."

"She's not paying for it. I am," said the man.

The Englishwoman looked out the window as Grace Church emptied out. His fingers lightly tapped the tabletop and his crossed leg moved to an imaginary beat as I placed the cup before her.

And I remembered a Sunday years ago. It was in January, a few weeks before Katie was born. Phillip, Michael, and I went to the park. We had just moved to Westchester. Michael was trying out his new hockey skates on the frozen pond, and Phillip was showing him some defensive moves. I walked along the path that wove around to the other end of the pond with Bridges; she was four months old. She ran out onto the ice and fell through, a couple of yards from shore. I knelt down and begged her to keep her paws up. All skating stopped, and I heard Phillip yell across the cold expanse, "That's a four-hundred-and-fifty-dollar dog."

The man brought back the Englishwoman's empty cup and asked how much I wanted.

"Four dollars and fifty-one cents," I answered.

The Wedding

Carole called from Westport. She and George had bought a house the month before, two blocks from the ocean. She wanted to raise the roof to have a cathedral-ceilinged master bedroom and bath. George refused. He told her if she wanted high ceilings to go to church.

"I don't know where to have Eloise's wedding. Do you have any suggestions?"

"Why don't you have it here?"

"Could we?"

"I would love it."

"It would be great, but what about Phillip?"

"Why is everyone always so concerned about Phillip? Jesus, it's my house too. It'll be a dry run for when Katie and Charlotte have theirs."

"I doubt if you'll still have the house."

"You never know."

"You better check with Phillip."

"I don't have to check with Phillip. There won't be a problem. Phillip happens to like Eloise."

"I just don't want to have any unpleasantness."

"What about George?"

"Anything he doesn't have to pay for is okay with him."

"Carole, I won't be able to pay for this."

"No, that's not what I meant. We'll just use the house."

"That's fine."

"No, everything else we'll pay for."

Phillip insisted they take out insurance, notify the police, and have Porta Potties available for the two hundred and ten guests. Poison ivy starts to turn red in September, and Charlotte and I spent a few days in long, heavy gloves pulling it out.

Eloise wore a white linen dress with silver-threaded butterflies and a wreath of flowering lavender and rosemary. She held a blue leather-bound book of poems that had belonged to her grandmother.

She walked with her parents on a path made of apple twigs. It began by the terrace and went past the pines into the clearing next to the apple orchard. Grape and bittersweet vines grew along the stone wall near the altar made of late summer flowers. Eloise kissed her groom, a young man with a trust fund, and the golden early evening sun shone on them.

Tables and a huge dance floor were set up under two joined tents. Zinnias, cosmos, and snapdragons were everywhere. Hundreds of glass jars, holding candles in pink sand flown in from Bermuda by George's army buddy, hung from the lower branches of the pines. The shadows danced along with the music of the Brazilian band.

There was a vodka bar and oysters on ice. Poached salmon, fillet, salads, champagne, and a rose-covered-cottage-shaped wedding cake. Eloise had asked me to make my carrot cake with cream cheese frosting, and Stephen and Sam made their chocolate cookies. The Brazilian band played while I sang a few gypsy songs. One of George's aunts ate two dozen oysters and danced the merengue and passed out. She wasn't found until the tables were broken down.

Katherine brought her boyfriend, Rob. Michael brought his girlfriend, Merille. And Phillip, wearing a black silk collarless shirt, pressed beige linen pants, and Armani sunglasses, looked as if he should have brought someone.

George paid the band to play another hour, and Katherine said she wanted to talk to me in private. We sat on the stone steps at the front of the house. I looked at her profile in the light cast by the table lamp next to the window. She told me she didn't know what to do with Rob. He and his mother got into a screaming match. Katherine was worried that if she stayed with him, he would treat her like he treats his mother. She was scared, she told him she loved him, she didn't want to hurt him. They had fun together, and he took her to these great places. Why couldn't it just be normal?

"Remember the night we went to the Palm for Charlotte's birthday? All of us were thinking about what to order for dessert, and Rob said he never ordered dessert. He said when he was a young boy, his mother would punish him before dessert, and she would send him to his room."

"Mom. I know. Isn't that so sad? I feel so bad for him, but what do I do?"

"Katie, you've got—" Suddenly Phillip was there, pointing his finger at Katherine.

"You're drunk, and you're disgusting. I saw how you were dancing, and you and I are going to have a talk tomorrow morning."

I stood up. "You're not going to talk to Katie that way."

"You know, Amine, you are a crumbling piece of shit."

"I know. Go to bed."

After he left, Katherine and I sat in silence until I said we should go back to the guests.

I Want a Tree

The police came in two squad cars. You could see the red lights spinning from the kitchen windows.

Phillip came downstairs and went with one of the officers to the room with the two Steinway grands to make a statement. Another officer came into the kitchen.

"Are you all right, ma'am?"

"Yes, I'm fine."

"What happened here, ma'am?"

"My husband said something to me, and I hit him."

"What did he say?"

"I can't repeat what he said, I'm sorry."

"That's okay, ma'am."

"Would you like something to drink or eat?"

"No ma'am, that's all right. Thanks."

"She says that to everybody who comes into the kitchen." Michael stopped smiling when I looked at him.

The three of us stood there silently and waited for the other police officer to finish taking down Phillip's statement.

A third officer came into the kitchen and told me if they had to be called back to the house again, both my husband and I would be spending the night in jail. Then he and his two partners left.

"Michael, come with me, please. I've got to get out of here."

"Okay, Mom. Just take it easy."

I left the kitchen to go to the front door as Phillip was walking up the staircase.

"Phillip." He stopped. "Aren't you ashamed of yourself? Aren't you ashamed?" He continued up the stairs.

Michael came up behind me and said he had to go upstairs to get his coat, even though he kept his coat in the hall closet.

"What did he say?" I asked Michael when he got into the car.

"Mom, he was in his closet crying. I never saw Pop cry."

"He should cry."

"Mom, enough. What did he say to you?"

"Nothing."

"Oh, okay. You slapped him across the face three times because he said nothing to you."

"Jesus. Why does he tell you?"

"What are you talking about? You tell me stuff. Hey, police are at our house, and you're worried that he told me you slapped him? Come on, this is getting fucking nuts. Why don't you both grow up?"

"I wish you wouldn't use the word *fuck.*"

"Right. Okay."

I pulled into the convenience store to buy a pack of Marlboros and a Dove bar; Michael didn't want anything and stood and watched me smoke.

"It would be better for everybody if he just moved out."

"Yeah, well, he doesn't see it that way."

"You know, Michael, after this I may be the one who has to move out."

"You have got to stop, Mom. Thank god Stephen wasn't here. Or the girls. That would have been a real nightmare."

"How are you doing? Are you okay?"

"What do you think?"

Sidney didn't hear from Nancy. From then on Phillip was away not only weekends but a few weeknights too.

I went into Phillip's room one night when Michael and Stephen were asleep. He was in bed reading, listening to Mariah Carey.

"Phillip, maybe you should think about moving out. You can get yourself an apartment in the city, and you won't have to go to hotel rooms anymore."

"Leave me alone," he said in a voice that allowed me to continue.

"I think it would be best for everyone. I'll stay here with Stephen, and you can come whenever you want."

"I don't want to talk about this right now."

"Phillip, let's just get this over with."

"Do you know how difficult it will be for me to move out?"

"I know, but we can't keep living like this. And you know it would be better if I stayed here with Stephen. We can't keep doing this to ourselves. You've got to concentrate on getting clients, and you'll be in a better position to do that in the city. Think of it like that, that you're doing this for your career. Don't think of it as leaving the family. This is your family. It won't just suddenly stop and be something else. I'll keep everything going here. There won't be this constant tension. I want to lead a happy and quiet life, Phillip. I know you do too. Don't you think you and I deserve it? Why don't you start looking for a place?"

"You dislocated my jaw."
"You shouldn't have said what you did."

Svetlana called and asked if I would come to Moscow for her birthday, the same day as my mother's. I told her I'd like to but I couldn't right now.

Phillip was talking on the phone through his closed door as I was putting away clothes Charlotte had left at the dry cleaner's. There was a two-inch space between the bottom of the door and the floor created during the renovation.

"We'll get a house.... Sure it'll be nice...."

"Do we need rugs?" "We'll get the best...."

"We'll have a tree?" "I want a tree...."

"Don't worry. I'll read or do something...."

"Yes, we'll take the Garden State. Bring the wine and vodka...."

The other phone rang. Stephen answered it, walked out into the hall, saw me lying on the carpet, and told Katherine I was busy. I went up to the attic.

At five in the morning, I went downstairs and knocked on Phillip's door.

"Can I turn on the light?"

"Yes."

I walked over to where he lay on his side by the edge of the bed. We looked at each other.

"I heard you on the phone last night, talking to her." He didn't say anything. "I was by the door. Phillip, I know you have someone. It's okay. Why shouldn't you? You're a healthy man, and we haven't been together for a long time. I'm fine with it. You're buying a house with her?"

"No."

"Don't lie. I heard you."

"It's a pipe dream. I don't know if I will ever again be able to buy a house."

"Phillip, all I have ever wanted was for you to treat me fairly. You say we have no money, and then I hear you saying you're buying a house, and I'm in ka-ka land. I don't know what's true. Phillip, what's the truth in all of this?"

He sat up and placed his feet on the carpet. He now wore tight briefs instead of boxer shorts. "It's a relief to have this out in the open."

"I have to go to Russia, my friend Svetlana isn't well. You have to give me money for the trip."

"How long will you be gone?"

"A week. Don't go away for the weekend—you have to be here for Stephen. And I want a video camera. Sony makes a small one."

"Okay."

"I'm giving Svetlana the mink coat."

"Do what you want."

Moscow was gray. There was a sprinkling of snow. The taxi passed people who seemed to be walking in slow motion.

Svetlana's apartment building was on Leningradsky Prospekt, not far from the Bolshoi Theater. She lived on the top floor in two rooms with a small balcony. You could see the red star of Kremlin Wall from the kitchen window. She was sitting on the couch when I came in through the unlocked door. She couldn't walk. "Don't be upset," she said to me. "Seventy years of dancing? What do you expect?" She rewrapped a large mohair scarf around her waist. She had on the cashmere slippers Carole had found at a thrift shop. She wouldn't wear the mink coat, she didn't go out.

Zina, the woman who swept the courtyard every morning, said she would look in on her. I bought a large bag of Tide and told Zina she could use it for everything. It was too expensive, she would never use it, she said; hot water and a good rag is all anyone needs. Svetlana wanted me to have the tea set she bought in Egypt, the cameo brooch that was her mother's, and the apartment. I sold the mink coat for one hundred thousand rubles to a woman I met in the elevator. I asked her to give it to me in twenty-ruble notes and told Svetlana to keep the money under the cushion of the couch she slept on. Svetlana said she would never be able to sell the tea set for what it was worth. I told her I would take it the next time. She saw that I didn't wear jewelry, and as far as the apartment, let's wait.

"It was 1956. I was here in this apartment. I had two rubles. I went out to buy something, potatoes, cabbage, whatever I could, whatever there was to buy. It was snowing, and it was starting to get dark. I saw an old woman selling sunflower seeds by the steps to the metro. I had seen her many times, I knew her son was an invalid, he lost both legs in the war. I asked her how much more she needed to sell before she could go home. Eighty kopecks, she said to me. I gave her what I had and didn't take the sunflower seeds. Came home. Later that night there was a knock on the door. A telegram. I was instructed to collect five thousand rubles for my choreography. The ballet was performed in Baku and Dushanbe to great acclaim. My father told me, 'What you have, you lose, what you give, you keep.' Always."

I came home from Russia the following Sunday. Phillip told me he found an apartment in midtown and that it would be ready by Christmas. We decided to put the house on Eel Point Road on the market. Nantucket real estate was skyrocketing, and we might as well take advantage of that. There was no point in keeping our furnishings there, it wouldn't help sell the house. Whoever bought it would be buying the property. Johanna said the house would most likely be torn down.

The Football Game

Phillip agreed that Stephen could play football, and Phillip and I were to watch the next-to-last game of the season. Stephen's freshman team was undefeated. He wanted me to get him up at six. "I have to take a shower. My pants will be ready, right? Be sure to get me up. Mom, do you know what I found out about today? You know Taoism. Right? There's no right or wrong. Right? Mom? I love you." He always says he loves me when he's leaving. He walked up the stairs from the laundry room.

Phillip and I sat at the end of the first row of the bleachers, away from the other parents. A young girl, the sister of a teammate, sat nearby, a small gray rabbit beside her. She fed her rabbit grass, a blade at a time. Kate used to do that. The girl's rabbit was on a leash; Katie ran after her bunnies.

It was a sunny, cloudless November day. The previous night's rain made a lot of the leaves fall. The men who came to do the fall clean-up that morning would still be there after the game was over. Some people had brought quilts to soften the seats, and many held containers from Starbucks or Dunkin' Donuts or from the deli at the top of the hill.

I'd had my chai tea with steamed soymilk. Phillip bought his coffee at the deli, probably from the woman who wears her blond hair up and who, when handing him his cup, smiles. He told me, once, when we stopped there on our way to the city to see Roberta Blanc, "Be nice. She likes me."

Stephen's team scored a touchdown. Phillip let the cellular phone in his left breast pocket ring.

"You better answer it, or she'll get nervous."

He smiled. The glare off of Phillip's dark glasses hurt my eyes, and when he stood up to walk to the end of the bleachers to talk to her, I switched sides. My eyes turned to Stephen. He kicked the football through the center of the goal posts for the extra point.

Phillip came back and sat down.

"If you need to leave."

"No, it's okay."

His phone rang again. He excused himself and again walked away.

I watched Stephen tackle the quarterback on the thirty-yard line.

"It's okay," Phillip said as he sat back down.

"I think it's good that you're moving to the city. Aren't you glad you won't have the commute anymore? You've decided not to take anything from the house, right?"

"By the way, I got a call from the Harvey Brothers. They're coming Tuesday to look over what's to be moved. And I told them all I want from Nantucket is the piano."

"Are you sure you don't want one of the grands?"

"Positive. It won't fit in the apartment. By the way, I think there may be a buyer for one of them."

"Are you going to give me half of the money if it's sold?"

"Sure." He smiled.

"What are you taking from the house?"

"My bed, I guess. My books, the CD player and my CDs, and my clothes."

"I want the dust ruffle."

"That's fine. I'll get a cheaper one." He looked out to the field. "Did you see that? He's really got great instincts." Stephen ran and again tackled the quarterback just as the quarterback caught the ball.

"Katie's coming home Tuesday night. Maybe you can take her out to lunch on Wednesday before she sees the doctor."

"I was thinking about doing that. She's going to be all right?"

"Yes. He says it's just a cyst, and it'll probably go away by itself."

Katherine had told me she told her father she'd help him furnish his apartment because he should have his own things there; otherwise, when she stayed with him, she wouldn't feel comfortable.

Michael told me his father told him Katherine thinks the apartment will become a home base for her and her friends and he's not going to allow that to happen.

I had asked Phillip if he was planning on setting aside a room for Stephen. He told me it was a small apartment.

"I think you should talk to Stephen soon."

"I know I should. I should have done it before. I'm just afraid he'll think I'm the villain in all this. I'm really nervous about it."

"He doesn't. None of them do. He asked me if you had a girlfriend, and I said yes and told him what little I know. He's fine with it because I'm fine with it. It's okay. It's natural that you have someone. Why not? What is there to feel ashamed about? I'm fine with the whole thing, and so are the children. Everybody's fine. There's nothing to hide anymore. Do you love her?"

"Yes. Maybe you should tell Stephen why all this came about."

"What do you mean?" Stephen kicked for another extra point. "Tell him about...?"

"That's up to you. I just think he should know there are always two sides to everything. He'll find out one way or the other. You always do." And he looked to Stephen standing on the side-line, drinking from a bottle of water.

She called again. Phillip went away to talk to her and came back.

"I don't have any more resentment toward you," he said, adjusting his sunglasses. "It's just gone."

"I think it's because you found someone else."

"I think it was everything. Yoga. Time. I was really destroyed there for a while. I'd sit at my desk and just look out the window."

Stephen tackled the quarterback on the forty-yard line. "Some day I'll have to tell you how I went hunting for a woman. I had to prove to myself I was still alive. I couldn't believe how I began to act. Me, who was so inhibited? I met a woman from Romania. She was thirty-nine. I liked her. She had someone hand-deliver a letter to me at the office. She wrote, 'You have to spend more time with me.' I took her letter and put it in the drawer of my desk and never called her again. She called me a few weeks later, and I said, 'Aren't you a bit aggressive?' And she told me a friend of hers told her to write that." He threw his head back and laughed. "Right. She told me she showed the note to her boss, and he said to her, 'Boy, are you stupid.' I stopped seeing her."

Stephen tackled the quarterback again. Three of his team-mates surrounded him. One gave him a high-five, another slapped him on his back, and the third put his arms around him and lifted him off the ground.

"Amine. You'll get yourself a fabulous guy, who's rich."

A week later, late at night, Phillip and I were in the front hall. I sat on the bottom stair of the staircase; I could see into the other rooms. Phillip stood across from me, his back against the wall, his hands behind him. Stephen had gone to bed early, upset at losing the last game. Michael was in the city staying at a friend's.

"The Harvey Brothers are coming tomorrow around ten, they said."

"I know. I'll be here."

"I've labeled everything. I told them what to do. You know that I don't want to be alone," Phillip said to the oriental carpet.

"I know."

"You were never there for me emotionally."

"You must have your phone connected by now."

"Yeah. I'll call you tomorrow, from work, and give it to you."

"I think I'm going upstairs to bed. I'm tired. I don't think I'll be up tomorrow morning when you leave for work."

"That's fine."

I was in the kitchen when the Harvey Brothers came.

"Mrs. Calt, how are you?"

"Fine. How are you, Paul?"

"Can't complain. You know Larry and I were just saying as we were driving over here, this has to be the ninth time we're moving you. It was New Hampshire and Nantucket. Nantucket was a few times, wasn't it? And then the city."

"There was also Bedford."

"Oh yeah, that's right."

"Phillip left everything upstairs. I guess he told you."

"Yeah, he faxed us."

"Paul, when you dismantle the bed, could you please take off the dust ruffle? You can just leave it on the floor."

"Yeah, Mr. Calt mentioned it. No problem."

It didn't take long for them to get Phillip's things out of the house. They were gone in less than an hour.

When they left, I took the blue porcelain lamp that was on Phillip's side of the bed to the hardware store to get it fixed.

"Mrs. Calt, how are you?"

"I'm fine, Mr. Hendricks. Mr. Hendricks, I don't understand this lamp. I've tried fixing it, but it doesn't work. I've tried tightening it from the bottom, I know that's what you're supposed to do, but you see how it gets? Just as soon as I think I've got it, it falls over. See how the bulb gets loose? See how it is? It burned the lampshade. I can't do it anymore. Do you think you can fix it?"

"Mrs. Calt, are you okay?"

When I got back, there was a message from Carole, on the machine. George was in a coma, to call her, and she left a number.

"Amine, we just had dinner, and we were going home. I had my back to him and I heard him fall down the steps, and you know how he clowns around, and I tell him to get up. I say George get up. And he's lying there smiling, and I told him he wasn't funny, to get up, and then I saw the blood and I started screaming. Oh, Amine, what is this? I told the doctor I don't want a vegetable. I have to go, I'll call you."

George died the next day. Carole wanted to donate his body parts. Everything but his liver, she said. It turned out George's liver was fine, and some man in Hartford, who's fifty-five, has it. Carole asked me to speak at his funeral.

"And could you say that I'm not dumb."

George's childhood friend spoke before me. He told us George had been drafted by the Chicago Bears, but he wouldn't go because he had just met Carole and she wouldn't leave her mother.

Carole embraced Phillip when we came through the receiving line.

The Norway Spruces

Michael moved to the city a few months after Phillip left. He has a studio in a sixth-floor walk-up on Third Avenue. He got a promotion. He rides his bike in Central Park after work. Katie designs jewelry and lives with a friend who she skied with in New Hampshire. Charlotte took an acting class during the summer and wants to go into theater. Stephen has a driver's license and a cell phone. He got an eighty-eight in economics and wants to be an architect. I've had Michael's paintings framed and hung throughout the house. Eloise took Carole to Paris. Coming back, the cab driver didn't take them to the right terminal and charged them seven dollars more after he took them to the right one. Carole told Eloise not to pay him, and he yanked one of the Hermès bags from Carole's hand and threw it into the trunk of the taxi. Carole got on the hood of the taxi and grabbed the windshield wipers, telling him she would rip them off if he didn't give her Hermès bag back. Eloise paid him, and they almost missed their plane.

––––––––––

In the fall I called Mr. Jenkins, who owns Horizontal Trees, and asked him to come to the house.

"Mrs. Calt, I don't recommend that you cut down these trees."

"They're too close to the house."

"They don't pose any threat to your house."

"I'm afraid one good storm will knock them over, and they'll fall and destroy the house."

"Are you kidding? Never happen. These are Norway spruces; Vikings used them for their masts. They don't get any stronger than this. Believe me, they'll be here after you and I are gone. It would be too sad to cut them down. I wouldn't do it."

"Mr. Jenkins, they don't allow the light to come in."

"You won't get as much light as you think, and you'd be surprised at the amount of noise and dirt they don't let in. I'll do it, but believe me, you'll regret cutting them down."

Phillip called to ask what we were doing for Thanksgiving.

"We're having it at home. You're invited."

"That's what I want to talk to you about. You know, I didn't take a vacation, and I thought I'd take this time to get away."

"Okay. That's fine."

"I feel guilty."

"Why? Don't."

"I can't help it. It's the way I am. We've always spent Thanksgiving together. Even when we were at war, we were together."

"It's all right."

"Who are you having?"

"It'll just be us. Where are you going?"

"Somewhere warm."

I called Mr. Jenkins and told him I had changed my mind. He was right, the pines shouldn't come down.